YOU CAN ALWAYS EAT THE DOGS
THE HOCKEYNESS OF ORDINARY MEN

JOHN B. LEE

YOU CAN ALWAYS EAT THE DOGS

THE HOCKEYNESS OF ORDINARY MEN

Black Moss Press
2012

Copyright © 2012 John B. Lee

Cataloguing information available through
Library and Archives Canada Cataloguing in Publication

ISBN 978-0-88753-513-0

cover photo by: The Culinary Geek
interior image by: Frank Woodcock

Layout & design: Kate Hargreaves

Published by Black Moss Press at 2450 Byng Road, Windsor, Ontario, N8W 3E8 Canada. Black Moss books are distributed in Canada and the U.S. by LitDistCo. All orders should be directed there.

Black Moss Press books can also be found on our website www.blackmosspress.com.

Black Moss would like to acknowledge the generous financial support from both the Canada Council of the Arts and the Ontario Arts Council.

 Canada Council for the Arts   Conseil des Arts du Canada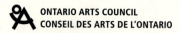

PRINTED IN CANADA

Work from *You Can Always Eat the Dogs: the hockeyness of ordinary men* has been published previously in: *The Hockey Player Sonnets: overtime edition*; *That Sign of Perfection: from bandy legs to beer legs—poems and stories on the game of hockey*; *Windsor Review*; *Kodar*; *Black Moss Press blog*; *Marty Gervais Poet Laureate of Windsor website*; and "That Sign of Perfection" was broadcast in a CBC radio documentary on hockey.

"Amundsen also planned to kill some of his dogs on the way and use them as a source for fresh meat."
A description of the intention of Amundsen's successful expedition to the South Pole, November 1911

"To become the man you want to be, you need to be in the company of men..."
Wayne M. Levine, in an interview about his book,
Hold on to Your Nuts: the relationship manual for men

"...Ultimately, the solution appears to be a balm that soothes many of life's problems. More hockey."
Rob Cribb, from the article
"What's wrong with men today?" *Toronto Star*

Dedicated in particular to The Skatin' Skolars, and in general to everyone with whom I've played pick-up hockey and to the memory of Ralph Evans, Ray Antoniolli, and most especially to the memory of Jamie Legacy, thank you to Frank "Woody" Woodcock for his sharp memory and his keen editorial eye, to my cousin Susan Scaman for her recollections of Andy Bathgate, and to my son Sean who still deigns to play with his dad, and to Cathy who encourages this pylon with words of kindness and love.

TABLE OF CONTENTS

That sign of perfection

Part I—born to the sign of the rain

Snapshots:
The lonesome egg	11
Born to the sign of the rain	11
A day that none can take away	12
Eating skaters' snow	13
The tragic collapse	14
Gentle but strange	15
Winter	17
Winter ii	18
When blood on the ice ran grey	19
Public skate	20
Driving on ice	21
NHL Power Play Tabletop Hockey	22
… a very embarrassing tryout!	24
A simple act of kindness—slew foot, the hook, and me	27
Quick study, slow learning, and starting again	29

Part ii—have you ever heard of a game called shinny?

Alive in the phone book	33
Nicknames: conversing with 'The Claw'	35
Einstein's hammer	39
Public skate ii	41
Public skate iii	42
'… never play hockey with an undertaker'	43
Wency's sense of water	46
Bumptious in the dressing room, quiet on the bench	47
Fighting—big dog, little dog, mad dog, fool	50
Goalies are different	55
Away Games	58
Injuries	62
The vocabulary of water	64
Remembering ice	68
Counting the loss…	69
Counting the loss ii	76
Tripped by Andy Bathgate	79
The swear jar—words with the flavour of soap	81
All those Christmases ago	82
I love hockey that much	84
In the end	86
A conversation gone awry	87

PART I: BORN TO THE SIGN OF THE RAIN

That sign of perfection

from bandy legs to beer legs
from kids hacking it out between snow-boot goals on ponds, gravel pits, frozen creeks, and backyard and schoolyard rinks
to old-timers grinding it out in pick-up games in the late-night arenas of little towns and big cities all across the country and for all the glory between
for the players with plenty of heart and soft hands
for the pylons and hackers who keep going though they have nothing to give but their love of the game
for the fathers and mothers up by five and out by six on the coldest morning of the winter
for their sons and daughters—
from wobble-skaters with their kitchen chairs to showboats and sharpshooters
for the netminders, for the blueliners, the centres and wings
for the spectators who watch and for the players who play
for what we remember and what we dream
this is hockey

Snapshots: the lonesome egg

I see my mom and dad were married in a home wedding on an uncommonly warm winter Saturday, January 8, 1949. After the ceremony in my mother's humble family homestead they went outside to be photographed in shirtsleeves on the lawn of the small hardscrabble farm a mile from Mull crossing. They set out from there in the dying hours of the day for the motor city where they stayed at the Lee Plaza hotel located in the shadow of the Olympia. The following evening, my father and his new bride watched a game between the Leafs and the Wings from the standing-room-only section of the arena. The game ended in a 2-2 tie, and Mother always remembered the pain in her pinched feet standing on the hard, unforgiving floor in her brand new high-heeled shoes.

Snapshots: Born to the sign of the rain

Two years later came the feckless child. Sickly. Ill-coordinated. Born between seasons. Born to the sign of the rain.

I remember myself as a one-legged skater, skating in a two-legged fashion of a skateboarder—one leg striding, the other leg gliding. I played my first game at six years of age in a New York Rangers jersey, jar rings holding my shin pads and socks in place, I stumbled onto the ice like Andy Bathgate's wobbly-kneed newborn calf.

Now I'm a man. I've played hockey seven times a week in winter and three times a week in summer. Sometimes I've played thrice a day, sometimes all day in the burning-cold wind. I believe in my heart that the promise of a perfect shining oval of freshly watered ice is one of the most beautiful sights in the world. I enter that wonder and thrill to the feel of first stride.

Snapshots: A day that none can take away

In my mind's eye I have an image of my father's laced-up hockey skates tethered together hanging from a spike hard hammered into the brick wall in the back shed of the farmhouse where he was born. I wouldn't swear to that location. And I can prove it neither false nor true because the new owners of the farm have leveled and removed the ruin of the shed and kitchen from the south end of the dwelling that was once our family home. Perhaps they hung from a nail on the outer wall of the horse barn, perhaps over the workbench above the vice beside an over-sharpened hoe.

The first artificial ice in my region became available with the opening (circa 1954) of the arena on Ridgetown agricultural fairgrounds six miles from our farm. Prior to that and for a few years thereafter, public skating and organized hockey was made possible by the flooding of community surfaces. In the village of Highgate, located a mile east of our farm, that responsibility was taken up by the men of the local volunteer fire department. They watered the cement floor in the school-fair building most winters during spells of reliable freeze. Before he retired his skates shortly after he was married, my father played hockey there for the village team. To hear him tell it, he was a pretty good winger. Something of a local hero. A hockey star of note. Never mind the braggadocio. Given the opportunity, I too can concoct lies about my own particular prowess. In my case, I usually undervalue my abilities and suffer the false humility of the quietly talented few. My younger son Sean says I'm a better hockey player than I say I am and most guys aren't as good as they think they are. How my father weighs in on the liar's scales I'll never know, for I never saw him play though I do suspect he doth exaggerate.

I recall my father skating only once, and on that occasion for the briefest while. It was a good winter day under a cold sun-blue heaven. The farm pond was well and truly frozen over on the surface of the east muck where the ice shone like a black-backed mirror. My sister and mother were there as well lacing up their milk-white skates for doing the mitten daub of figure eights. I'm not actually certain that my mother ever skated. But she's there in this fond memory of that nearly perfect day when I was six or seven and full of the impossible joy of being alive in the body when the body first discovers new things.

In the big barn there hangs a smock for ghosts. On the silo door a toxic warning of death behind the wall. The cattle yard is tall with weeds. The top rail of the bull fence sags on rot like a wind-broken branch. The eaves refuse to hold the rain and the foundation stones have tumbled into rubble at the base. The hay is white with lime and the empty darkness has no hunger for the light. Those skates my father wore have gone the way of mortal objects into dust. But in memory as in dream they remain as real and I see him skating on a perfect morning long ago. A day we shared that none can take away.

Snapshots: Eating skaters' snow

For a few winters even after the arena opened in Ridgetown, I would throw my laced-together tube skates over my shoulder and walk the mile to the village to take advantage of the last of the natural ice in the township. If I recall correctly, there was a public skate every Friday night in the dead of winter. We sat on makeshift benches set at the south end of the building and laced up our skates. In a throng of skaters we played the forbidden game of ice tag. Without benefit of music we went round and round in a random carousel. When we grew thirsty we simply scooped up a handful of skater's snow and slaked ourselves with that.

It tasted of street dust and mitten wool with a slight fragrance of moth balls in the yarn and with a touch of ice-grey in the snow-white—it sufficed in the two-hour thrill, skating round and round and round until the clock ran down and we all walked home under a glorious dazzle of winter stars.

Snapshots: The tragic collapse

On February 28, 1959, the Listowel Memorial Arena collapsed, burying a boys' hockey team playing a scrimmage game—the worst tragedy in the town's history. Seven young players, along with a referee and recreation director (Reginald Kenneth McLeod), were all killed in the tragic collapse.

I was small for my age when in September of 1958, my father decided the time had come to sign me up for house league hockey. I was born in November, barely eligible for making the cut as I wouldn't turn seven till the grey month of chill rain. In Gladwell's book, he quotes a coach who said of his son he was always big for his age. What that coach didn't realize was that his son wasn't actually big for his age, but rather he was old for his age, and being born in January had made him a full-calendar year older than some of his teammates. When you're in the middle of your young life you are most likely unaware of this unfair disadvantage.

The better players receive more coaching, more ice time, more practice, more play and the lesser fall further and further behind. This advantage manifests itself in a likelihood of making the majors. As it turns out, a statistically significant majority of NHL and Olympic hockey players are born between January and June. In one particular list, over eighty percent of the team was comprised of those born in this period.

My father had bought me a New York Rangers hockey jersey, and I arrived at the arena, the puniest boy on the team. I'd learned to skate on the ponds at home on the farm. But I had a weird stride pumping my right leg and keeping my left leg steady. I suspect I skated that way because my sister and I shared a single roller skate left on the farm by our city cousins. It was a key-skate attached to the sole of the shoe, and we had only one skate that fit on the right shoe. We had no left skate and we'd take turns going up and down the el of the veranda wearing that four-wheeled skate on our right foot and pumping away with the left leg. And so, that's how I'd learned to ice skate as well. It would be one full season of hockey before I managed to correct my stride and use both legs in doing so. In my own mind's eye I can see myself racing down the ice, one leg madly pumping away, the other leg riding a groove.

It wasn't long before I was sidelined by sickness. I had a predisposition to pneumonia and I soon succumbed to the annual bout of being bedridden with high fevers and shallow breathing. I don't recall much of my hockey career that year. I'm not even certain I managed to play a single game.

However, I do have a vivid recollection of a tragic event pertaining to hockey that sad season of my first year as a young player. In the winter of 1959, on February twenty-eighth, the roof of the Listowell arena collapsed during a scrimmage smothering seven young players along with their coach. I don't recall how I learned of this tragedy. I certainly didn't read the newspaper, nor did I listen to the radio nor watch the nightly news. I suppose I might have overheard my father mentioning it at the table.

I imagined those boys suddenly smothered by falling rafters, my young life haunted by images of those doomed youths who perished mid-stride buried forever under the horrifying beauty of deep snow.

Snapshots: Gentle but strange

The boys with whom I played hockey during my two years of house league were total strangers to me. Even now I cannot recall a single face or name. I think I must have dressed for the games at home, because I cannot see the dressing room in my mind's eye. I see myself arriving in full gear with my head warm in a blue-and-white wool toque typical of the period. Those were the days before helmets. I suspect I am correct in thinking of myself arriving, driven the five miles to the arena by my dad, crossing the parking lot on my way to the big door wearing grey-white skate guards fixed in place by sheathed springs. Occasionally a player forgot to remove his guards and he would take a dramatic pratfall stride splaying out and sliding like a calf on a pond.

I don't remember a single practice. I don't remember one game. I don't remember a solitary coach. I do have a vague recollection from the beginning of the season of my second year when an adult made the observation that the small boy out there doesn't know the meaning of offside.

Even now, there's one particular wag with whom I play. He's ten years my senior with an exaggerated idea of his own meager talent. I often hear him from the opposing bench shouting that I'm offside. And although he's only half joking, I know he thinks I do not know the meaning of the term. Very recently, he took me aside after a game and attempted to give me a skating lesson involving the cross-over. I paid attention for a few minutes as he instructed me, demonstrating what he wanted me to attempt as if it were a difficult dance step I needed to learn. I gently explained to him that I could not be coached and that it was far too late in life for anything like a skating lesson. I had to smile after a game the following week when I witnessed him giving a similar mini-lesson to another fellow.

Listen, I overheard him saying. I've been watching you skate and I've always wanted to show you something …

This same fellow and I were once briefly engaged in a conversation on the bench awaiting our shift as linemates on the ice. Being friendly by nature, I asked him if he was enjoying his recent retirement and what he liked to do in his spare time. "I like to read," he said.

Since I'm an avid reader I pursued the topic with enthusiasm. "What do you like to read?"

"Non-fiction mostly, history and philosophy."

"What history is your favourite?"

"I like ancient history. Roman and Greek history."

"What philosophers do you enjoy reading?"

"I like anything. Mostly Greek philosophers. You know. My favourite is Socrates."

I wasn't being pedantic and I meant no harm, but I made the error of saying, "Actually, Socrates didn't write a single word. He was a great teacher, but it was his student Plato who gave an accounting of his master's lessons."

"Why don't you shut the fuck up and concentrate on playing hockey. I'm not here to talk. I'm here to play."

I was taken aback by his anger. I suppose to be fair I must have seemed like something of a know-it-all. I should have taken that exchange as a sign that I must treat this fellow gentle but strange. He's a bit of a bruiser, chippy on the ice and grumpy on the bench. I can well imagine watching him as a youngster taking a faulty stride having forgotten to remove his skate guards, and I smile to think of him stepping lively, slipping and spilling, his body spinning like a bottle in a game of kiss the girls.

Now I think back on my own early linemates, those imaginary strangers, and I realize that they would have been my classmates in high school, my catechism contemporaries the year I was confirmed in the church. Perhaps those boys with whom I played were the same ones I came to know well. Surely they would be. This was a small-town arena, and mine was a small-town school. Whoever they were, wherever they are now, they were strangers to me then during those two short seasons of house-league hockey. I never played organized hockey for the next fifteen years. I never learned the cross-over on the way to my hapless career.

Snapshots: Winter

Winter is my favourite season. Is now, and always has been. Every year in the late autumn I have my annual "first snow" dream. That lovely surreal weather comes to call in the December darkness of deep sleep. As long as I can remember, I have felt a primordial longing for the hibernal beauty of shorter days of early sundown and the coming on of clear black star-dazzled solstice under cold heaven.

I learned by reading that in the years of my childhood growing up in the sixties that this had been the coldest decade of the century. Coincidentally, Dickens' childhood had been similarly cold with snow in the streets of London and the frozen-over Thames of the *Christmas Carol* years. Little wonder then that I recall a time of deep ice and plentiful snow.

The ponds and creeks, the gravel pits and farm reservoirs, the lakes and rivers were frozen for months on end. I remember walking the mile to school in the village with the snow banked and looming like sea cliffs on the road shoulders. A boy could climb those white gravel-stippled slopes and he might stride along the crest of those berms whose peaks were threaded through with telephone wire buried at the post tops.

Winter brought me two of the great loves of my young life. February delivered the Beatles to our farm parlour when I was an impressionable twelve-year-old lad on the cusp of puberty. But long before that, winter carried with it the possibility of hockey.

Snapshots: Winter ii

Every winter on the farm, low land might flood and then freeze. The hog wallow under the elm just over the fence from the shed door, the cow pasture west of the house, the gravel pit across the Gosnell line, the twin mucks at the bottom of the hill on either side of the banked-up lane near the road, ten acres of perfect ice if that water froze on a windless night. I skated on them all. The hog wallow was small, but it was sheltered and close enough to the house to enjoy a quick and solitary skate.

Some days a few of the village boys would wander down to the farm and we would play shinny all day long, skating with that hard-hollow *cut cut* sound that comes only from natural ice. If it snowed, we scraped a rink-sized surface, sometimes making a five-shovel crew, sometimes taking turns when there was only one shovel to be had. Sometimes we played in a white dusting of new-fall so the puck slid over a darkened path. Sometimes the ice would crack under our weight and send a crooked black line slithering along the surface. Once or twice over the years, one of us would fall through when the ice collapsed because we hadn't tested the thin spots. When we inadvertently found these danger zones we'd set out a wool mitt warning. If you weren't careful you might stumble onto white ice and crack through thin shatter as if you were skating on barn glass.

I've played alone for hours, carrying the puck and imagining glory. I've played with a single friend and I've played with multitudes. It was always best with eight or ten. More made for too many, fewer and the game went back and forth too fast. We never got cold. We never grew tired. Losing the light we sometimes surrendered to the darkness. But a full moon might give us just enough of a white glow to continue after supper. Never mind the burning wind and sub-zero cold. After fifteen minutes of play, no matter the chill, we'd shed our jackets, lift our toques to the hairline, toss our scarves to the wind and skate. As I think on this I can almost hear the hard woody clack of the stick slapping the puck so it spanked into snow-boot goal posts and then spun away. A week into our play, the water supporting the ice would seep away and great sheets would collapse on their own weight and cave in like roof rot on long-abandoned buildings. And that was certain to be the last of the good days.

Snapshot: When blood on the ice ran grey

I am essentially a television baby. Many of my earliest memories involve grey-fleshed cowboys with twin six-shooters slapping their thighs, singing from the saddle to the lazy clip-clop accompaniment of white-maned horses with high-groomed tails sweeping the air against sunset backdrops as they moseyed under the arched gates of the home ranch, raising a little whirl of dust in their wake, strumming an orchestral guitar and yodeling about a wild west that never existed. Saddle tramps and sugar foots. Sidekicks and masked heroes. Roy Rogers. Gene Autry. Jingles. The Lone Ranger. Red Rider. Gabby Hays. Rusty and his good dog, Rin Tin Tin. Bullet. Trigger. Champion. Nelly Bell the jeep, with Pat Brady for comic relief fast-talking behind the wheel.

When I was old enough to stay up past seven, I joined my father on Saturday nights where we gathered as a family to watch hockey on TV. My sister, my mother, my father and I watched only two shows together. One was *The Ed Sullivan Show* on Sunday evenings and the other was

Hockey Night in Canada. My wife Cathy also remembers her own family ritual when her dad made maple sugar fudge during first intermission, a sweet treat they shared over the second period of play. For my family, Saturday night was a night for buttered popcorn popped between periods in a black-bottomed frying pan, and a single glass of Coca-Cola served on ice in faded green aluminum drinking glasses that were chill to the touch.

    Dad's first memories of televised hockey involve gathering at Stub McPhail's garage where the men crowded round the first TV in the community. He recalls Rocket Richard, wild eyed, feral, his forehead beribboned by blood, driving for the net, cheered on by the roar of the crowd as he carried the nation on his shoulders, accompanied by the frantic voiced announcer shouting "He shoots! He scores! A scintillating drive!"

    I don't watch televised hockey very much these days. Haven't watched much since childhood. Indeed, I don't really enjoy watching sports on television. Truly, I never have enjoyed it much. But I did love being together with Mom and Dad and my sister on those popcorn-fragrant winter evenings long ago, when the excitable Danny Gallivan called the play and I lay on the parlour floor watching Dad taking each single satisfied sip of stubby-bottled ale, hearing that advertising jingle, "Hey Mable, Black Label" with a blizzard whirling in darkness outdoors.

Snaptshots: Public Skate

    The first time I heard "Day Tripper" I was upstairs in the Ridgetown arena lacing up for the high school's public skate on the last afternoon before Christmas break. It was December 1965 and I was a grade-nine Poindexter on the cusp of a profound obsession. I was just beginning to notice the opposite sex.

    The song opened with a trademark guitar hook and the famous Beatles were mine alone. That John Lennon riff went deep and we all woke up. The DJ dropped the needle in that torpid groove and Paul began to sing. I looked up over the last tight tug of my laces snugging at my ankles so the aglets clicked and—I saw girls.

It was an age of mini skirts and go-go boots, an era of bottle-blondes with poker-straight Peggy Lipton hairdos and sweet sweater curves in soft swells of mohair. Girls in their wool-white socks and their shiny toe-pick skates, some in leotards, some in flesh-hued hose, and some bare-legged and blushing in the promise of cold.

I stood an inch taller than myself and walked ticky-tack on the toes of my blades onto the ice entering the grand skaters' carousel. There would never again be a first time for hearing that song when I was fourteen, and the Beatles were mine, and my interest in girls was brand new.

Snapshots: Driving on ice

I loved skating so much that once I had my license I started driving to the arena on Saturday nights. Even though I drove alone, skated alone, I didn't mind at all. Better that than lonesome nights isolated on the farm in the long winter darkness. I loved walking past the hot dog counter with its spiced meat and mustard aromas and the scent of steamed top-cuts rising from the opened bin of fresh buns. On the ice I raced round and round, flashing past couples, wind whistling in my ears. The music was almost always current: The Beatles, The Stones, Motown—Smoky Robinson and the Miracles, the latest hits from the hit parade. I imagined the girls watching me. Even though I hadn't played hockey much due to poor health in my younger years, I was becoming a very good skater. Fast. Sure on the corners. Weaving through the crowd without so much as brushing a single scarf or mitten. Me in my navy-blue, brass-button military pea coat feeling so body wonderful in the full vigour of my youth.

It would be that same year, the year of my last months in high school, when I started playing hockey again, learning to put my skating skills to even more joyful purpose. Beginning my lifelong affair with pick-up hockey.

Snapshots: NHL Power Play Tabletop Hockey

"...madness is repeating the same action over and over again and expecting a different result."
—*Albert Einstein*

One of my favourite Christmas recollections goes to 1957, the year my sister and I had a sleepover at our cousins' home during the holidays. The Gardiner family lived in a frame house set on a sandy-soil farm. We were best friends with our cousins who lived a life that would seem old-fashioned even by the standards of the day. They had an oak wall-mount hand-crank telephone with a candlestick receiver, hand-pumped cold-water kitchen plumbing, a square galvanized washtub, and an outhouse.

That year cousins Bill and Alan received an NHL Power Play tabletop hockey game from Santa Claus. It had a scoreboard arching over centre ice. The team sweaters on the tin players were those of the Toronto Maple Leafs and The Montreal Canadians. The puck was placed on the bridge of the scoreboard so it dropped onto the ice when you shook the game. A long metal rod with a rubber grip on the end manipulated each player except for the goalies who were attached to a flat metal lever. We set the game up on the dining room table and played for hours in the dry interior heat of that winter house. Slamming the rods home. Ramming the goalies, our thumbs bloodied from the frequency with which we jammed the mechanism under the nail, hammering the net minders so the puck shot over the faux ice like a flat black bullet. We played until the dining room table was worn raw where the game rubbed away at the hand-darkened varnish. We stabbed our palms defending the honour of the defence; we gored our hands for the wingers' want of a goal. We played all afternoon and evening, dreamed of glory in our sleep, and resumed our play in the morning until noon. It was a battle to the end. Sudden-death overtime. We were Canadian boys in love with hockey. Ice hockey, field hockey, floor hockey, road hockey on tarmac, on gravel, on grass, and tabletop hockey.

I didn't have my own game until my wife bought me one as a gift the second Christmas after we were married. That same year I started playing pick-up hockey with a teachers' team called *The Skatin' Skolars (sic)*. We took to the ice every Monday afternoon at four where we played for an hour in the Waterford arena. My enthusiasm for tabletop hockey revived and deepened along with the opportunity to play ice hockey. As twenty-three-year-old newlyweds, my wife and I lived in a big old drafty brick farmhouse with a huge country kitchen. We set the game permanently on the harvest table at the centre of the room where we played most afternoons following work and then all day Saturday and Sunday. We shared the house with an American poet named John Paul Reidl. John Paul worked at the local wool factory, played hockey with the *Skatin Scolars*, wrote fine poems, played guitar, and joined us at the table for tabletop hockey marathons. John and I both became proficient practitioners of those rod-manipulated skaters. We took on all comers. We blistered our hands and bloodied our nails until we broke every spring in the game. After living there for a year, wife Cathy and I moved out leaving that nearly destroyed game right where it sat at the centre of the table in the centre of the room.

A few years after our children were born, my wife bought a new improved tabletop hockey game for my sons and I when they were old enough to play. By that time I was pretty good at playing. I could beat almost anyone. But my boys weren't that interested. They were of a video-game generation. And they were good at that, far better than at tabletop hockey. Having grown up with my game, I could easily defeat them. The scores were lopsided in my favour. However, when I played video hockey, I was pathetic. My younger son in particular could easily defeat me, running up a score of twenty or thirty to zero. In fact, I'm not certain I ever scored a single goal against him. My players were either in the penalty box for accidentally tripping their opponents, or my goalie was out of his crease mindlessly banging the boards behind his net with me shouting, "Why is he doing that? I don't understand this game. Why is my goalie banging the boards with his stick like a lunatic?" Meanwhile, Sean would be laughing his head off at me, popping the puck into an empty net, and mocking me at centre ice, racing away with the puck again and again, my goalie repeating his actions like Einstein's madman.

Snapshots … a very embarrassing tryout!

I don't remember my sister or any girls ever playing hockey on the ponds. When we boys went down to lace up our skates and play, the girls seemed either to be absent or they were there in their ultra-white figure skates with toe picks digging in doing figure eights on the sidelines while we scrimmaged and scrambled after the puck.

I recently wrote my sister just to confirm this recollection and she certainly set me straight. Not only did she play hockey, but also she tried out for the girls' hockey team in high school. She tells me she did not make the cut because she could not skate fast enough with all that equipment on. It was a very embarrassing tryout for her. All her best friends made the team and she didn't.

My wife Cathy did make the girls' high school hockey team at Central in London when she was in grade nine. Although she was a good athlete from a very athletic family, her brother being an all-Ontario track star, Cathy was also very small for her age. She was what one might call a pipsqueak. She was tiny, even by female standards of the day. At four-foot six, weighing in at less than one hundred pounds, she stepped onto the ice like a little female Pocket Rocket—more moth than behemoth on skates. Since there were no other teams in the area, they played a single exhibition game against the Mustangs girls' team at the University of Western Ontario. She doesn't recall a single practice. When I asked her recently what position she played, she replied without missing a beat, "Survivor." The university team members seemed like giants in her recollection. On first face-off she overheard one of the Amazons cautioning her teammates, "Don't hurt the kid." She said this gesturing toward the grade nine pixie, the Tinkerbelle on ice who would one day grow up to be my wife, the love of my life, and the mother of our athletic children.

Years later, when both Cathy and I were hired to teach at Waterford High School, I was asked to join the staff hockey team *The Skatin' Skolars* for their weekly Monday afternoon scrimmages. Excited by the prospect of playing hockey again, when Cathy expressed a strong desire to join us she was flatly refused. "Women aren't welcome," someone said. "This is a men's team. If you want to play, the women play broomball once a year at Christmas." And so she did not play. She simply wasn't allowed. And that was that. I didn't realize it at the time, but she was truly hurt. "Would you have played if you had been allowed?" I asked. She immediately said, "Yes." And I'm slightly ashamed that I did not press the point at the time. Especially since the teachers' team had so many feckless, spindly-legged skinflints who could barely skate. We had a Poindexterish physics teacher, a bandly-legged stumble-bum art teacher, a gangly Ag teacher, a business teacher who played in dress pants, a guy who stuffed a towel under his helmet and who looked like Herman Munster on skates, a half a dozen guys who skated like marionettes with tangled strings. Oh, we were hawks and sparrows indeed. Mostly sparrows. A few of the hawks were quite good. And I am certainly no hockey player. Am not now, and never have been.

I'm not proud of the fact that I didn't stand up for my wife. I played with those guys for over thirty years. I remember most of those years quite fondly. But as I look back on this one issue, I'm reminded of how exclusive a club we were.

Over the years I did play with a few women, but never on that team. I played with a group of guys from the Deaf Blind unit from the W. Ross MacDonald School for the Visually Impaired. We played every Friday afternoon from four until five p.m. On one occasion early in the game, a new player took a run at me giving me a full body check that slammed me hard into the ice. Being a relatively gentle guy, I picked myself up and went on with the play. Then a few seconds later, the same stranger skated half the length of the arena and banged into me sending me reeling, my stick flying in the air, cracking into the boards ten feet away. Once again, I stood up, brushed away the snow from my hockey pants and resumed play. When this individual came at me a third time, I stood my ground, set my skates firmly in the ice, found my best centre of gravity, and hip checked the oncoming player, bouncing the offender off my body. The helmet took flight, arms and legs affected a star shape and spun across the rink as the gloves detached and shot off in opposite directions. One of the guys skated over and gave me a piece of his mind saying, "That's a girl, you know. Amber. She's new on staff. You shouldn't treat a girl that way. What kind of guy are you?" If I am correct, that was the first last and only occasion that Amber ever played with us.

There were a couple of girls who played varsity league hockey that took to playing with us when I was on a team in Simcoe. They were both easily the best two players on the ice. The one girl didn't come out too often, but her friend played with us for about two years. They dressed in their own dressing room, kept pretty quiet on the bench, and just mostly did their job on the ice. One of the men on that team, a guy named Monty, whom we all called the coach, because he was so inclined to give advice though he never seemed to take it, used to congratulate Amy all the time. "Way to go guy. Great shift, guy." He'd even say this when she sat right beside him on the bench. I'd overhear him saying to her, "Great passing out there, guy. Keep up the good work, guy." Finally, after several months playing with her, I said to him, "Monty, (we never actually called him coach to his face since we meant it as an insult), that player you keep calling 'guy' is actually a woman. She's a nurse in Simcoe. Her name is Amy." When he gave me a blank look, I added. "Didn't you notice that she never dresses in our dressing room? Take a good look at her the next time you sit next to her. Look at her face under the mask. You'll notice she wears makeup. She has long hair and she wears lipstick and eyeshadow."

"No," he said. "I don't believe you." Whether he believed me or not, I never heard him ever call her 'guy' again.

My niece played hockey when she was a young girl. She loved the game. However, the time came when there were no further opportunities for her to play. My cousin Helen played senior women's hockey in Aspen, Colorado. She was always quite a sporty girl, and although I never saw her play, I suspect she was probably quite a good hockey player. On one occasion when our ice time in Syl Aps Arena in Paris was preempted by a girls' league, the guys grumbled for months afterwards. Why should women be allowed to jump the queue? We'd been playing in that ice time for ten years.

As for me, I'd rather not enter into the gender wars. I champion human rights on either side. But if I have to come down on one side or the other, I'd have to agree with those who champion women. I wish I'd come to my wife's defence when she was refused an opportunity to play on the teachers' team. I wish I'd remembered my sister's non-existent hockey career. Now forty years hence, when I close my eyes in an effort to see my wife as a niner, I conjure the image of her with a hockey stick in her hands, her body swaddled in her older brother's protective gear, skating my way, hammering me to the ice, driving for the net to score.

Snapshots: A simple act of kindness —slew foot, the hook, and me

In grade thirteen I met lifelong friend Gary Schatte. He had moved to Ridgetown from London. He owned a car. A Rambler. He was a great organizer and we shared many enthusiasms. We both loved music, especially The Beatles. We both played chess. We formed a chess club and became vice-president and president respectively. And Gary arranged the rental of the ice at the local arena so we played pick-up hockey once a week for an hour after school. I don't think we wore much equipment. A stick and a pair of skates seemed to suffice. I owned a pair of skates and a hockey stick I used for grass hockey at home.

The year we rented the ice in high school, I was certainly one of the least skilled and least experienced players in my graduating class. But

I could outskate almost everyone. I wasn't much good at lateral moves, but I could go from skating forward to skating backwards with great ease, as long as I didn't hit a groove or a rut on the ice. I can still skate backwards as fast or faster than many of my fellow players. Of course, youth and stamina and real hockey players send me to school, but I'm still as good as the best and better than most when it comes to pure glide.

That said, I developed two compensatory moves to make up for my general lack of skill. The year we rented the ice in secondary school, I perfected the slew foot and the hook. Of course I didn't know that these were both dangerous and illegal moves.

I'm still slightly ashamed of the time I threw the slew foot, tripping my good pal Henry Aukema, so he fell mid-stride in my wake. He came up swinging, not at me, but at Gary whom he'd thought guilty of the infraction. It was I who had dragged my trip foot in his path. To this day, I'm ashamed to admit that I allowed Gary to take the heat. Henry Aukema's rage cured me of the slew foot, a move I'd tested and found wanting.

The hook, on the other hand, remains in my arsenal. Only a few years ago, when I hooked Hank Hare's stick with my stick, the blade inverted over the shaft of his, thereby hooking him off the puck, he turned and lashed out with his Koho. He lay siege on my wrists and forearms indignantly cutting his way through my pride screaming by way of demonstration, "This is a HOOK! This is not a HOOK!"

Apparently he was righteously angry and seemingly legitimately aggrieved. Near the end of the season, he apologized. But I've been told that sometimes I should be more careful since some guys don't take too kindly to being hooked.

Snapshots: Quick study, slow learning, and starting again

I left my childhood behind the autumn after the summer the Beatles broke up. Something of a late bloomer, I started university in the fall of 1970 as an innocent farm boy. That year I'd lived inside the seventh circle of hell, a two-tower residence at Western in London. Officially known as Saugeen-Maitland, the students called it the zoo. No mentors. No elders. No mature guides. No cautious or wise counsel—just nine hundred boys and six hundred girls gone wild with the self-destructive freedom of youth.

That same year I played hockey twice. Once when we rented the ice in the city. And once when I went to the tryouts for the intramural residence team. Feeling mostly the joylessness of physical exertion and the extremely obvious and self-evident limitation of my own comparative abilities, I abandoned the game for the next five years. Neither the opportunity nor the desire to play presented itself until I joined the staff of Waterford District High School in my first year of teaching.

PART II: HAVE YOU EVER HEARD OF A GAME CALLED SHINNY?

Alive in the phone book

I had neither skated nor played hockey since my last few forays in the late fall of first year university, and I had gone from being a whippet-thin hay-strong youth to being a whip-armed bandy-legged twenty-three-year-old Poindexter with nothing to recommend me but desire. A few of the male members of the staff at WDHS had established a pickup hockey team calling themselves *The Skatin' Skolars* and by the time I arrived they were two sweaters into their mandate as a Monday-afternoon league. They were a rather motley crew ranging from a few ex-pro leaguers through wobble skaters who could barely stand. Sieve, the goalie wore paper-thin equipment, but the shots were so often wild and wide of the net that sometimes the safest place on the ice was between the posts. Boom-Boom was so named because he fell down every time he took a shot. The art teacher, Babe skated willowy legged as though his ankles weren't paid for. Scooter Scovil was a sickly ninety-pound weakling with a worm he'd ingested while teaching in Africa. One or two of the originals had given up the game and surrendered their sweaters, so I snagged a blue sweater from one of the quitters. I was without experience and almost completely devoid of talent. I fit right in as a middle of the pack player. We had Ralph Elbows Evans, a.k.a. 'the silver fox' so named for his handsome features and silver-grey hair. He had played serious hockey in his youth, and if you let your guard down he might make you regret the lapse in attention. The Red Wings had scouted Al Hagerman, but though he had all the skills necessary for big-league hockey, he lacked the killer instinct and I heard he'd chosen to quit pro hockey in order to get married. Stretch a.k.a. 'grumpy' was a six-foot-seven physical education teacher. If he fell on the ice you might hear someone cry "timber" without being ironic. A great group of guys with a long history, I played with them for almost thirty years before I decided to move on.

Although we sometimes played in tournaments and engaged in officiated games with refs and whistles and the structure of three-period stop-time contests, I always preferred the wide-open fun of a freewheeling scrimmage. The high point of our bonding as a team came the year we organized a game against the NHL Old Timers. Another apotheosis came at Guy Johnson's wedding, when we formed a circle, arm in arm and sang along to Willie Nelson's song *On the Road Again*. That song had become a theme of ours when we first sang it in the bus on the way to Wheatley for our annual away games at the teacher's tournament. We drank together, sang together, conspired against authority and farted our way through several decades of fellowship and fun. The sillier we were, the more fun we had. Playing with those guys reminded me of how much I loved hockey. So, I played the game every opportunity I had.

By the time I was at my peak of playing, I played seven times a week on seven different teams in winter and three times a week in summer. I played Mondays with the Skolars, Tuesdays with a group of pilots in Paris, Wednesdays with the cardiac league, Friday mornings with an over-fifty group I joined when I was forty-three, having left full-time teaching when I was thirty, Friday afternoons with the Deaf Blind Unit from W. Ross MacDonald School for the Visually Impaired and Sunday mornings with Wes Stewart and his family. When the Stewart clan hits the ice, Wes can suit up an entire team without going outside of the family gene pool. I played regularly in Waterford, Simcoe, Brantford, Paris, St. George, Norwich, Ancaster, Cambridge, and Burford. I played in the Shade Street Arena, reputed to be the oldest established artificial ice in the world. I played in Plattsville where the dressing rooms were upstairs and you had to come ticky tack down the steps to get to the ice. I played in the Ancaster Double rinks where you had to skate around the detritus from the ceiling for fear of tripping on falling insulation. I played in Dundas where you had to skate uphill on a sloping surface in order to exit from the ice. I've played in Midland, Penatanguishine, Coldstream, Wheatley, Langton, and London. I've played when the ice was summer soft and thick with fog. I've played through power failures with the doors thrown open for the benefit of daylight. Now I play three times a week, twice in Port Dover, and once a week in Waterford. I've limited myself to playing in an over-fifty league. The oldest guys are in their eighties, and the young fellows are my age or younger. For a while in the early days of my latter-day playing, I was among the best players on the ice. That was when I was at the top of my game. The first occasion of my playing with the old fellows in Waterford on Friday mornings, I scored fifteen goals. But there were guys there then who were old enough to be my grandfather. One fellow had been an Lancaster bomber pilot in WWII. He came out to scrimmage even after he'd had a stroke and his left side didn't work just right. Now, I usually score one or two goals a week. I'm in the middle of the pack again. I've broken my leg and my nose. I've chipped a tooth and popped a knuckle. I dislocated my pinky finger so that when I took off my glove, I noticed my finger pointing my way like a cocked open shotgun. Seeing my distress, friend Al Hagerman told me to look away, as he snapped my finger back into place. I taped my glove so the last two fingers were secured together, and I went back on the ice the next shift, and I played that way for the next two years. I've had orthoscopic knee surgery to repair an old injury from childhood. I've shoveled my way to the rink and driven home through blizzards and sleet that would send a sensible man to the nearest motel. I love pickup hockey almost as much as I love my marriage. I hope I'll know when to quit. But I'm not there yet. A friend of mine recently said of our hockey playing colleagues, "some of them are still alive in the phone book." And I'm wondering if I won't be playing as long as I'm alive in the phone book. I see my name there still, and I think *Leapin Lee* has another game in him yet.

Nicknames: conversing with 'The Claw'

We called him "the claw." He could pick anyone up on a dare using only his middle finger looped through your belt buckle. He challenged all comers. We'd lie flat out on the floor of the staff room and he'd lift each stiffened body craned by the hook of his swear finger so you would seem to float towards the ceiling like a magician's assistant at a magic-show levitation. One by one we subjected ourselves to the test. The entire hockey team: Mad Dog, Rocket, Woody, Wheels, Zippy, a.k.a. the big Zee whom I called 'Zed' out of respect for my Canadian roots, Scooter, Zamboni, Guy—pronounced in the French fashion with a hard 'g' and a double 'e' as in Bee, as in Guy Lafleur, Fat Boy, Elbows, Stretch, Reboot, Wacky Wallace who carried a knife, Dead Eye who was blind on one side, and me, Leapin Lee. I was last. I floated, up, up, one inch, two inches, no part of my body touching the tile floor, cap-a-pied, rising, rising, floating with a lightness of being as if I were buoyantly drifting in warm water and then with a snap my belt broke and I collapsed in a clatter. The Claw triumphant, his pinky finger raised like a delicate tea drinker, his strong finger triumphant. It was my belt, not his digit that had given way.

And that is how it was with us. The Claw, who'd given up playing hockey before I had joined the staff, was still on the team, and he would always be part of the team. I'd seen a photograph of him in his green jersey from the sixties when everyone was younger, young and full of the vigour of youth. That was when Sieve was in the net, when one guy named John was Babe, and the other guy named John was John Paul. Everyone on the team was reborn, renamed, rechristened.

If you were on the hockey team, you were given an apt sobriquet. You were never Doug, or John, or Ralph, or Frank. You lost the name you were born with. Joining the team involved a christening. In the early days, electricity teacher Jim Ross became Shock, Don Giles became Don B., John Gresko became Broken Leg Gresko, Phil Cook became Cookie, Al Hagerman became Whirling, and coach Tom Wardlaw became Paunch, so named as an obvious variation on Punch Imlach and in deference to his own rather generous belly. Later in the Skolars' history Paunch served as honourary coach and the new coach was a guy we called Slick. Slick had a silvery mane he slicked back and held in place with a generous lathering of hair tonic. Frank Woodcock became "Woody." I called him Paco Coq du Bois, but that name didn't stick. Being clever with collective nouns and knowing that a gathering of woodcocks is called a fall of woodcocks, I said of Frank who frequently fell to the ice, not because he is a poor skater, but rather because he's inclined to risk himself by going full out in the game, "When one Woodcock falls, Woody, do you still call it a fall of woodcocks?" I'm shameless that way, laughing at my own jokes. When someone took exception to a player spitting on the floor while sitting on the hockey bench, I said for my own amusement and fully expecting not to be understood, "What did you expectorate? He's a spittin' image of his own father."

Every team I've ever been on seems to rename certain players. I play with a line we called the red army simply because they wear red jerseys. One fellow we called Bondo because he owns and operates an autobody shop. Another guy's Stewey—a name he prefers to his given name because his last name is Stewart. There's 'the sidewinder', and 'Bushel,' the submarine man 'up periscope,' and 'the coach' so-called because he's always full of the gall of unwanted advice. There's 'the train' who carries the puck, hogs it all the way down the ice from behind the blue line at his own end, his stick going *click clack click clack click clack*, never passing, never looking up, never giving way. Someone once brought a train whistle and blew it from the bench while the train chugged past, his cage like a cow catcher on a steam engine, guys chanting 'chug-a-chug-a' and 'Woo! Woo!' It wasn't exactly a 'get off the track / here comes Eddie Shack' moment, more like a runaway diesel rushing full bore for the roundhouse, and nine out of ten times just at the last moment the train would lose the puck to an opposing player who would then easily break out of the end thus rendering the entire drama meaningless. Sometimes, I'd simply stop where I was, lean on the boards, blow my nails and wait until the train had completed his useless routine. At the end of one season when he received the annual "Puck Hog Award," no one was surprised but he. He sees himself differently. Actually, most of us do see ourselves differently if we see ourselves at all. And thank goodness for that. If we depended upon hockey for our self-esteem, we'd be weeping most of the time.

And there's—"hey Abbot," there's Bull, and the Iron Man, a lantern-jawed guy whom we'd all thought of as indestructible until the day he was seriously injured in a car crash. There was a goalie who called himself Super, and he shouted in warm ups—"Shoot the puck at my head! Shoot the puck at my head!"—banging his cage with the flat of his stick like a zookeeper waking the lions. We took to calling him "Headshot," after that. There was Nebuchadnezzar the young guy with the Old Testament haircut and long black beard. Plugs of Red Brand chewing tobacco also blackened his teeth.

There was "Misha" whose given name was "Misha" after the Russian Bear. He didn't need or require a nickname. He was a Friesian kid who, though he could barely skate was always fast. Being speedy, completely out of control and slightly mad, all at the same time made him a most dangerous force of nature. He skated like he was drunk, or high, or as if he were being chased by killer bees, or by cops, he skated like a man with stones in both shoes. No, Misha didn't need a nickname. He was just Mish. Eventually he moved away. I heard he is living in Toronto and that he's making a living as an elevator repairman. Perhaps he still plays hockey. I don't know. But if he does, and if he ever learned to skate, I imagine he's still something to watch, zooming down the rink like a whirlwind on ice.

There are a few guys who still go by their given names. There's guys whose names I've forgotten long ago, and there's guys whose names I never learned. As for me, I was called "Leapin'"—a name given me by the daughter of my former department head. When I was a young teacher just starting out, she saw me on the ice at the first annual Christmas hockey game and called me "Leapin' Lee" because to her young ears that name was euphonious, alliterative, affectionately descriptive, and it would do the trick for a guy who had no name. Some guys call me "Johnny." They don't know, but that is the name my sister still uses. It's a name I haven't answered to since childhood. My good friend Roger Bell calls me "Bust" when he's in the mood. That's my own private Rumpelstiltskin of a secret name, my middle initial being 'B' and my middle name being a well-kept secret. Only a few people know what the "B" stands for in my name John B. Lee. The

Claw is one of those few. He's a man gifted with an elephant's memory. A polymath. A mad mathematician with a Rosicrucian's knowledge of arcane things, an inventor, a deep thinker, and a lover of conundrums beyond the ken of most, he tinkers in probability, he concerns himself with game theory. He's a man with a barn full of lathes and he owns forty-seven hammers, no two hammers having the same purpose. As I write this, he is working in a yellow yard waging war on pissabeds.

Why not be the peen and not the claw—I joke. His answer is complicated and wrong.

Einstein's Hammer

When my son Sean stripped the puck from former Leaf captain, hockey superstar Doug Gilmour, during the NHL Oldtimers' exhibition game in Hamilton, Gilmour simply hooked him in the belly, pulled him backwards off his stride so he was left skating in place as though in suspended animation like Alice of *Alice in Wonderland* who discovered that she must run faster and faster just to stand still. It seemed a surreal moment, with Sean watching Gilmour as though in a dream, as the superstar lifted the ostensibly magnetized puck from the ice so it hovered on the flat of his stick, swirling it in the air like spun sugar, skating down the ice as if the puck were glued to the lumber, bedazzling everyone with this prestidigitation, (now you see it, now you don't) as in one smooth motion he twirled the blade and dropped the puck over the goalie's shoulder behind his back and into the net, thus scoring a magnificent goal to the amazement of the net minder who was so mesmerized by the entire affair he failed to move a muscle. Great athletes are truly gifted people with extraordinary talents and physical skills beyond the ken and experience of ordinary mortals.

I'm an ordinary mortal, but I wear expensive equipment. I don five hundred dollar skates and some of my teammates carry two hundred dollar hockey sticks. Like the pros, we too are armed with the best technology that sporting goods stores can supply. I once joked with a fellow hockey enthusiast who came to the dressing room preparing to don a brand new pair of high-tech hockey skates, "Isn't that a bit like putting Michelin tires on a wheel barrow?" We all laughed, but we also knew that the skates are only as good as the skater, the stick is only as good as the man. I wear expensive skates, and I'm not a bad skater, though I've seen how real speed and quick efficient bent-knee low-gravity-stride lateral-motion skaters leave me in their snow. Faster than most guys my age, I also know my limitations. I'm able to skate backwards with alacrity and ease of motion, and I'm able to follow the play and to stay with most of my peers to prevent the opponent from driving straight for the net. But I've played with one guy who can skate sideways faster than I can skate straight ahead. The best skaters are effortless. They are usually moving far faster than they appear to be for they have developed an easy efficacious stride.

    The hockey stick is an equally important piece of equipment. I'm something of a cheapskate, and so I rarely pay more than twenty dollars for a stick. My lumber is more than often made almost entirely from wood, and as a wag once chided from the bench, "Look at John Lee, he must be the last guy in the world with the same stick he used as a boy on the pond." Truth be told, anything more expensive would amount to an unnecessary extravagance since I suffer from what experienced hockey players call stone hands. Spending hard-earned cash on anything more costly would be a foolish investment. My advantage on the ice rarely involves my stick handling. My shot is hard, but seldom accurate. My passes tend to be sent on their way throat high. And I find it almost impossible to receive a pass on the fly. My advantage on the ice, if I have one, is my intelligence. I'm thoughtful. I play a thinker's game. A fellow player's praise for me, "You're one philosophical bastard, aren't you John?" echoes in my mind. My problem, my major shortcoming as a hockey player is in the execution of a play, not in the lack of well-considered intention. Though my mind is sharp, my body fails me. My eye-hand co-ordination is abysmal. I lack what is called 'puck sense'. I have to see the puck to know its whereabouts.

The best players simply feel its presence. I have to look down, witness its whereabouts, and thereby confirm my possession, but of course by that time I've been stripped and withered like a lonesome tobacco stem after a killing frost.

Though my hockey stick might wait for a Gilmour, Gilmour never arrives. When I take up my lumber, I celebrate the hockeyness of ordinary men.

Public skate ii

I bought my wife a new pair of skates for Christmas and we went ice-skating at the outdoor rink overlooking Horseshoe Falls. Every turn we took we caught sight of the puny rubble of the American side, that pale cousin to the emerald roar and raging mist of the far-more famous, far-more majestic Canadian cataract. As I caught sight of our falls, I thought of José Maria Heredia's poem, "Niagara," and my own translation from the Spanish of those lines, "sublime terror … prodigious torrent … frightening thunder … furious hurricane … boiling whirlpools … " came to mind. My Cuban friend and fellow-translator Manuel came to mind, and the day he and I visited Heredia's home in Santiago de Cuba came to mind. My wife and I, my son Sean and his new bride Bo, skating near Niagara, near the place where the doomed disappear on days of lost faith and dark despair, near the place where Nancy Lacko's daredevil uncle dropped over the edge in his barrel and entered the eternal shame of his forever-embarrassed family. We skated there, round and round, the coloured lights illuminating vapour like the rainbow hallucination of ghosts from another time. I thought of the young Joseph Willcocks picnicking on the rim of the green river with his elder beau Elizabeth Russell sitting together on the grass above the falls two hundred years before the evening of this day. I thought of the terrible battle fought here in Lundy's Lane with a thousand dead to measure the horror of local war. And of the sneer of horses dying in battle wild eyed in the primordial fires of night. If Heredia were here with me now, I wonder what he would make of the carnival on the Clifton Hill with its gimcrack museums and Count Dracula's castle doorway screaming at the street. And what would the great Hollywood beauty Marilyn Monroe think of us, skating in circles, laughing and loving this winter night under invisible starlight.

Public skate iii

Every Thursday morning since Christmas, my wife and I have gone for a public skate at the local rink in Dover. It's mostly a time for athletic geriatrics, cotton-top women, and balding septuagenarians too old for hockey, too young for the bone yard or the stale indoor air of slept-away mornings. Today, one old fellow in an antiquated pair of tube skates clung to the lip near the glass and shuffled along the wall like an ankle injury on his way to the dressing room. Either he had not learned to skate or he had not skated since childhood. Someone brought him a cheater and he staggered behind it pushing it over the ice like an old man toddling a nursing home hallway. For an hour we skated threading the pack, taking in snippets of overheard conversation. The man with the walrus moustache exhaled, voicing strong opinions on what needs to be done to improve the doomed and ever-lamentable Toronto Maple Leafs. Like all armchair coaches, he took vigorous strides, goating the circle bleating solutions, "Leafs this … Leafs that …" My wife says, "Maybe the other teams are just simply better." And then, there are the money talkers retired in privilege and hating the poor. There's the quiet ladies out on their own, widowed young, white hair bobbed, alive and ready for the long life in a world without men. There's the backwards guy, racing around in steady self-assured ovals, never looking over his shoulder, smooth and certain and easy as a Caribbean sea crab, he's that good in reverse, like a daredevil driver weaving through pylons in a fast car. He breezes around the ice without so much as brushing a single one of us. After the skate is over I ask if he ever played hockey. And I'm not surprised to hear his affirmation. He mentions five or six local names and I know them all. He gave up playing the game years ago. Doesn't remember why. It just wasn't fun anymore. Industrial League tough guys, mean-spirited rock-jawed men with something to prove, men who'd rather send you to hospital than surrender the puck, and pickup leagues, well, that meant too many late nights, too many early mornings tired at work. You know how it is?

And on the ice, exactly thirty minutes after the half-time flood, the skaters changed direction. For weeks I've been watching the crowd and listening for a signal that has never come, trying to discover whom it was that decided to turn and go the other way. Who is the bellwether; who is the powerful stranger whose lead we follow?

In Cuba, the week before, I'd found myself explaining the word bellwether to my fellow writers. Of course a few of them knew the meaning, but none the derivation. As a boy-shepherd in childhood I've always known a wether as a castrated ram and a bellwether as the cut buck wearing a bell in the wilderness. He's the one the flock follows, the one whose whereabouts the shepherd knows. Like the Judas goat in the slaughterhouse, he leads the way.

Next week I'll watch the skating crowd. I'll look for the powerful stranger. The first one who turns us all. Perhaps one day, it will be me.

"… never play hockey with an undertaker!"

I've played hockey with people from all walks of life. I've played hockey with teachers, professors and lawyers, with doctors, surgeons, nurses, X-ray technicians, homeopaths, quacksalvers, chiropractors, dentists, dental hygienists, and dental plate makers. I've played for years with a denturist who made his own dental plate. He lived in Toronto, where, because he was a pretty good hockey player himself, he was sometimes called upon to make false teeth for a few of the players on the Toronto Maple Leafs hockey team. "Whatever for?" I asked him when he told me that. A proud octogenarian tin-miner's son from Cornwall, England, I asked him if he still had the impression he'd made for General George Washington. "You bastard," he said, laughing his incisors into his open hand.

I've played with pilots, auto mechanics, airplane mechanics, guys who owned body shops, guys who sold sporting goods, guys who rebuilt engines, and guys who customized vintage cars. I've played with police officers, firemen, jail guards and ex-cons convicted of kiting bad cheques. I've played with deep-sea divers, real estate agents, social workers, interveners, and clerks. I've played with CEOs of international corporations, bankers and box-store owners and small-time entrepreneurs. I've played with multimillionaires and guys so down-on-their-luck poor they were barely able to raise the funds to cover their own ice time. I've played with cheapskates and spendthrifts, with farmers and hands hired to milk the cows. I've played with booksellers, poets, with artists and dancers, with scholars and guys unable to write their own name. I've played with navy men from two wars; I've played with a Lancaster bomber pilot, a submarine serviceman, and a veteran of battleship duty in World War II. I've played with speedsters and pylons, with fit youths and with guys refusing to quit even after they've had debilitating strokes. I've played with guys who've had heart attacks and guys who've gone under the knife. I've played with triple bypass survivors, guys with knee replacements and brand new state of the art prosthetic hips. I've joked with one fellow who has two artificial knees, one artificial hip, partial dentures and a hernial tuck, "If you add the age of your body parts to your chronological age and divide by four, you're easily the youngest man on the bench. George, the next time you get a new knee, you should have it motorized. Then imagine how you'd skate."

I've played with NHL hopefuls, with ex-pros and with guys who are still in the big leagues. I've played with them before they were called up and after retirement. I've played with Junior A, Junior B, and Junior C players, with rep-team players, with OHL score leaders, and I've played with the not-quite-talented-enough sons of talented fathers. I've played with Rob Blake, Jason Cullimore, Rick Wamsley, Dwayne Roloson, Chico Mackie, and Nelson Emerson. Nelson was a student in my grade nine English class when I taught at Waterford. I've played against old timers Ron Ellis, Norm Ulman, and Andy Bathgate to name a few. My claim to fame involves being tripped by Andy Bathgate, but that's a story for another chapter. I've played with guys who wear eight hundred dollar skates and who carry three hundred dollar sticks. And I've played with guys who still wear the same helmet they wore in Peewee. I play with a guy who stuffs a towel under his helmet so it will sit high enough on his head so he can see. I once played with a car salesman who never tied his skates. He took to the ice with the tongue flapped forward and his skate laces loose like my dad in a hurry on the way to the barn. And even though he never tied his skates, claiming he had great maneuverability that way with his ankles slopping around as he pivoted on the ice, he still changed his skate laces once a week saying, "I like the look of brand new laces." I'd probably still have two or three pairs of his discards in my hockey bag if I hadn't lost them in a move. I play with a guy who wears protective glasses with the lenses removed. I play with a guy who washes his skivvies and airs out his equipment between every game, and with guys who don't even bother to take their equipment out of their bags. Sometimes their long johns come out frozen cardboard stiff and the frost steams up from their skates.

    I play with oceanographers, plumbers, electricians, factory workers, priests and ministers. I once asked the priest, "Father Paul, who does God favour when you shoot the puck against Larry?" Larry's a Methodist pastor who plays goal. And I say to Larry, "If Bill is an atheist and he scores against you, does that shake your faith?" The reverend Larry favoured the wearing of a slightly sacrilegious T-shirt emblazoned with an image of Christ as a hockey goalie, his glove hand snapping a puck with "Jesus Saves" silkscreened under the hockey-playing messiah. Some joker snatched Larry's shirt when he wasn't looking and with a black-ink pen inscribed a caret between the 's' and the 'a', inserted a superscripted 'h' and then returned the shirt to Larry's bag so the next time he wore it, it read "Jesus Shaves." And as if to prove the truth of that claim, the same fellow had scribbled out our Savior's beard. Larry didn't notice, but when someone pointed out the corrected elision Larry had a good laugh, though I don't think I ever saw him wear that shirt again.

I've played Industrial League, No-Body-Contact, tournament hockey, and hockey that's just a scramble of guys so haphazard it seems that the ice must have been tipped in the direction of the play. As I say, I've played with all walks of life. Good fellows and some guys you'd never wish to see again. But I've never played hockey with an undertaker. Perhaps I've heeded my dad's frequently given fatherly advice. "Son," he'd said to me at least a dozen times. "Never treat women with disrespect. Never bring the police to my door. And remember this well. Never ever play hockey with an undertaker!" And I've always been a dutiful son.

Wency's sense of water

I have stood upon the sturdy vault-thick ice of a frozen bay and seen the skate scarring of that snowy surface, that white scrimshaw looping out like the trace lines of a much copied-over napkin. And I thought of this beauty when I mentioned ice to my Cuban friend Wency as we sat in the torpor of a Caribbean sun on an Island beach in front of Hotel Tropicoco located twenty minutes by car from Havana and the warm sea spray of the Malecón. It occurred to me to ask, "Wency, have you ever seen natural ice, outdoor ice, a frozen-over puddle, pond-ice, or lake-ice, or any ice at all other than the ice cubes you might use to chill your drink?" And he said, "No." Simply, "No." At this we sat in silence looking across the hot blond sand of the beach, from there out over the aquamarine waters and beyond that toward the imaginary shores of far-away America. His world, my world, our two worlds meeting, and though I might order a drink 'con hielo' I could not give him the gift of my winter. The lovely long ice-bountiful winters of my childhood would remain a mystery we could not share.

Bumptious in the dressing room, quiet on the bench

"never argue with a fool…"
—*Mark Twain*

Most of the guys with whom I've played hockey over the years have been men of few words. Rock solid types, ordinary stalwarts of good character, quiet men who keep their opinions to themselves. Taciturn fellows, who remain laconic and are often difficult to draw out. One player in particular, says little more than, "Yup. Nope. Maybe." Mostly he just shrugs and smiles when he's engaged. Once when I accidently tripped him saying, "Sorry Stan," he replied, "Sorry doesn't cut it." That's the longest speech I've ever heard him make.

However, there exist in every dressing room on every team of which I've been a part, a loud and opinionated few who can be counted upon to shout down all contenders and who consistently confuse the volume of the voice with the quality of the argument.

Although I've rarely experienced a real quarrel in the dressing room on one occasion when things were getting a little hot, one of the more vociferous participants turned to me, confronting my silence, inquiring with a big shit-eating grin on his face, "So, what does 'the poet' think?" I smiled back saying, "You really don't want to know." And he rejoindered, "Yes, I do. Tell me what you think of what we've been saying." Suddenly careless of his feelings and fully expecting him to take offence, I said, "I think this conversation amounts to little more than an exchange of ignorance." I was totally surprised when, rather than take umbrage at my insult, he gave a full-bellied laugh, clapped me on the shoulder saying, "That's good! I never heard that one before. Now I know what a poet thinks." I still don't know how he knew I was a poet, since I'd kept my avocation entirely to myself.

Then there was a time when one guy was waxing on about teachers. For whatever reason, politicians, lawyers, and schoolteachers seem to come in for the most unbridled criticism amongst amateur hockey players. All politicians are corrupt. All lawyers are liars. And all teachers are lazy good for nothings. The favourite quotation of such teacher bashers is, "Those who can, do. Those who can't, teach." And I've even heard it said, "Those who can't teach, teach teachers." The underlying argument seems to be that since everyone has been a student, everyone is an expert on the foibles of the pedagogical profession. This fellow was standing in the middle of the dressing room after the game, holding forth on the laziness, the greed, the arrogance and worthlessness of those who teach school. It wasn't his first dithyramb on the failings of the profession. Finally, having had enough, I interrupted him asking, "Monty, when was the last time you were in a classroom?" One would have thought I had slapped him in the face with a duelling glove. He puffed himself up, took in a deeply indignant breath of stale sweat-stinking air, and directed a red-faced tirade in my direction, "I have a right to my opinion! No one cares what you think. I'll say whatever I want, and you … you … you …" he sputtered out. Someone else, goggling at the floor said, "C'mon guys, lighten up." I could not help myself, it seems, though the better angels of my nature were fanning their wings in favour of silence, I said, "Monty. Indeed, you do have a right to your opinion, but the next time you share your view it might be more courteous of you to know what you're talking about." With that, Monty stamped his foot and was gone, slamming the dressing room door with a bang. Good-hearted Larry gave quiet council as he stowed away his goalie equipment, "John," he said, "you should let Monty have his say without comment. You have to know that no one here pays him any mind. You need to learn to just let it go. He has a lot to say, but we all know he's a blowhard. You, of all people, should know better than to respond. You basically called him a fool. And though he is a fool, and we all know it, there's nothing to gain by calling him out." Wise council indeed.

Once, while getting dressed for a game in Paris, one of the players was raging on in a very similar rant of teacher bashing. "My father," he blustered, "was a janitor in Burford High School. He made a tenth of what teachers make. He worked long hours cleaning up messy classrooms and cluttered halls. Most teachers arrived just before the nine o'clock bell and left for the day just after three. They have three breaks over the course of a six-hour day. They only work four hours a day five days a week. That's a twenty-hour week, not counting assemblies, school trips, and PD days. And then they get the summers off, and every freaking holiday under the sun, not to mention March Break. They only work ten months of the year. They teach the same lesson plans for thirty years, and then retire when they turn fifty with the best pension plan in the province. They're all a bunch of good-for-nothing whiners. My dad worked his fingers to the bone cleaning up their messes, and he made slave wages."

Nick finally paused to take a breath, and I'd simply had enough. He knew I'd been a teacher. I'd taught for fifteen years before leaving the profession to write full time. Perhaps I was still teaching at that time, I don't recall. Exasperated by his unchallenged oration, I finally said to him, "Nick. If your father resented teachers' salaries so much, why didn't he just go back to school, get himself an education, and become a schoolteacher himself?"

Here again, just as it had been with Monty, Nick reacted as if I'd slapped him in the jaw with the stiffened gauntlet of a wet-leathered hockey glove. He turned beet red, glared in my direction and barked, "You! You ain't nothin' but a fucking poet! You never broke a sweat in your life."

Realizing that he'd taken umbrage on behalf of his father, I said, "Nick, I certainly didn't mean to insult your father. Why would I do that? I don't even know your father. Please, I apologize."

"Why don't you just shut the fuck up!" he commanded. I happily complied, wishing I hadn't said a thing.

One of the goalies, meaning well, interjected, "I agree with John." Whatever that meant, it went unremarked.

Bud, who ran the hockey in Paris said, "C'mon guys. Lighten up. We're just here to play hockey. This is supposed to be fun. Leave the quarrels at home, or stay home."

Nick happily resumed his teacher bashing. I kept quiet. A few guys nodded in redneck assent. For my part, I thought of Mark Twain's caveat, "Never argue with a fool ..." and I might have presumed to add—

when you bother to argue with a fool, then there are two fools arguing. I felt like a mouth with no ears. And that is a man I do not admire.

Fighting—big dog, little dog, mad dog, fool

I've been spat on, choked, slashed, blind-sided, bum-rushed, tripped and chased around the rink by goons intent on mayhem. I have been in two fights in the last thirty-six years of hockey. One involved stepping in to save an asshole from being pulverized by a six-foot-five behemoth. The other involved being head butted by an anger management poster boy who went into therapy the following day. I have only retaliated twice. I refuse to follow the common hockey player's adage: *don't get mad; get even.* In my world, that sort of old-time-hockey, Don Cherry attitude amounts to idiocy of the worst stripe. I'm more inclined to turn the other cheek.

Let me tell you about Hector. A guy, described by everyone who knew him as such a nice fellow off the ice, quiet, calm, gentle, a family man, the brother-in-law of one the regulars, turned into a nasty piece of work the moment he stepped on the ice. With a dirty and grueling intensity, he hooked, slashed, chopped and boarded his way through every game. Ironically, in addition to being the dirtiest player on the ice, he was also the most talented athlete. He possessed every skill but the skill of self-control. He could skate, stick handle, pass, receive a pass, carry the puck, shoot and score, but he could not seem to resist indulging in completely gratuitous and unnecessary bullying of the opposition. Two of my friends quit playing simply because he would not let up. My best pal, Jamie the bookseller, lifted his shirt to show me the liver-coloured bruising on his belly where Hector had hooked him whenever he'd skated close enough to receive this calling card.

The first time I ever met Hector I made the mistake of asking him if he found it ironic to be playing in a town called Paris? On another occasion when he was grumbling in the dressing room, I said to him,

"Stop hectoring, Hector!" He didn't crack a smile. I don't believe he knew the history of his own name. Perhaps he hadn't read *The Iliad*. I dare not mention his Achilles heel for fear he might think I was being sarcastic. I do manage to amuse myself sometimes, though I suspect my wife is correct when she says to me, "You're just not funny."

Being a relatively gentle guy, and being disinclined to physicality, I chose to confront him directly concerning his infamous Hector hook. After one friend had quit, and another friend was seriously considering giving up hockey, and because I'd had quite enough of it myself, just after the time Hector shot the puck deliberately at my head for having been slightly stale on a pass, I decided to confront Hector in the dressing room. I waited until he was seated and comfortably disrobed, I rose, crossed the floor, stood toe to toe, looked him in the eye and said, "Stop hooking! Do you understand me?" Hector seemed cowed by my words. He stared at his feet, acquiescent, seemingly contrite, almost whispering, responding sotto voce, "Sure, John. Sure." I know I'd shamed him, though I was to learn the following week just how wrong I was to have done so.

He came out onto the ice even worse than before. After the third or fourth infraction, smarting from an absolutely gratuitous hook, I'd simply had enough as I spontaneously threw a hip check catching him off guard and knocking him into the boards right in front of our bench. He hit the wall and flew apart like a Volkswagen in an accident. His helmet took flight, his gloves shot off in two directions, his stick leapt from his hands and went clattering, he fell and spun spread eagled as though my right hip had detonated a hair-trigger charge set deep in the core of his body. I immediately regretted what I'd done, but a cheer went up on our bench, and Nick patted me on the back saying, "Good for you, Johnny. It's about time somebody rang his bell. Maybe it will teach him a lesson he won't soon forget." Quiet Mark congratulated me, saying, "He deserved it. I'm surprised you put up with him for so long." His brother-in-law Gary said, "It's the only thing he understands." And for the rest of the time we played together, he not only left me alone, but he became so very 'buddy buddy' it was embarrassing. Our relationship from then on was like a big dog little dog cartoon friendship. I never did come to like the guy, but at least he stopped the infamous belly hook whenever I skated near him.

I'm ashamed to say that that was not the only occasion when I stooped to disgrace myself by betraying the better angels of my nature. The worst player on our team in Paris, a guy equally incapable of self-restraint, but a guy so entirely devoid of talent he did not possess a single skill and he seemed unable to learn. He had no understanding of the game, no insight into his own bottomless incompetence, and he was reckless and given to thrashing after the puck like someone trying to kill a rat with a rake. He indulged in every bad trick he could manage. If you dared to skate near him he'd lash out with the blade of his stick as if he were grappling after a big fish. He fell often, usually taking one or two other players down with him. One time after I had already passed the puck, he continued to make me dance scything away at my ankles as if I were a patch of weeds he meant to destroy, and eventually, I turned around, stuck my blade in his skates, pulled, and down he went. He came up thrashing. He caught me on the back of my calf with a blow wielding his Koho like a sword too heavy to handle. I lost my cool and swung, knocking him off his pins and sending him limping and wincing to the bench. That may be the first, last and only time I have ever struck a blow in anger against another human being.

I didn't retaliate then, and I didn't retaliate when Mike Vice spat in my face. I hadn't responded in kind when one goon with a criminal record to his name skated after me, chattering in my ear about what he'd do when he got me in the parking lot. I told him to shut up and play hockey. When Vice had spat on me, Ian asked me on the bench what I'd said or done to provoke him. I told him Mike had taken exception to my having tripped him. When I assured him it was not I, but another player who had committed the infraction, he told me to "Fuck Off!" I'd responded by saying, "No, Mike. I won't fuck off." Then he repeated, "Fuck off!" And I said, "No, Mike." Again. And when I said 'no' he spat in my face. Ian said, "No wonder he spit on you, John. You can't say 'no' to a guy like Mike. You should have just said 'fuck off' right back at him. Then he would have respected you." That's hockey logic.

Even when Mad Dog put me in a chokehold for stripping him of the puck, and then skating past him I didn't retaliate. Mad Dog grabbed me by the sweater from behind, put his stick across my larynx, pulled the stick tight on my throat, and although I could feel the rage surging through his arms, I just stood there waiting for him to follow through. When I could feel his arms relax, I turned around and said, "What is wrong with you? Are you crazy?" I could see by the glazed look in his eyes that he had mental health issues. He confessed to me that he'd taken rage management for years and that if not for the success of that program he might have killed me. "He's too dangerous to know," is the way someone put it a few years later, after shunning his company.

As I said, I've been struck twice in an entirely one-sided hockey fight. I'm what Don Cherry might call 'the poetry guy' when it comes to his notions of real men. The first fight I was involved in was on the occasion when I stepped in so a guy we called 'the coach' wouldn't be pulverized by a six-foot-five inch Neanderthal. The coach is a snide, lippy, unlikeable, pencil-necked fellow. He probably deserved to be struck, but I just simply couldn't pass by without a calming comment. I didn't like the odds. The coach had been sniping at a not-so-gentle giant at the end of the game, and so they were squaring off for a knockdown. There was bad blood between them, and truth be told, there was bad blood between the coach and nearly everyone with whom he had ever played. But I could not skate away and mind my own business. I skated over to where they were squaring off, the coach sneering and needling, his moustache twitching, his pipe-cleaner arms twiddling, as the behemoth was clouding over for a thunderstorm of whoop-ass. I stepped in and said, "C'mon guys." Goliath turned to look my way thereby focusing his rage on me, and with one quick jab, punched me in the cage, knocking me to the ice. The coach took full advantage of this opportunity and beetled away and into the dressing room leaving me to contend with the Yeti. I got back on my feet, as the big guy prepared to hit me again should I dare him to do so. I looked at him and said, "You sir, are a behemoth. You are a Neanderthal." With that, I departed for the dressing room. He came sputtering in after me. "What did you call me?" "I called you a Neanderthal. A behemoth. An abomination. Grendel." Needless to say, he departed. And I'm not proud to think of how I behaved, though I'm pleased to remember that I did not hit back, at least not with my fists.

The other time I was struck, it was by a guy named Neil. Most of the time, Neil was a pretty good guy. But he was reckless on the ice and indifferent to the danger he caused because of the way he played. He left a swath of bodies in his wake, not because he was particularly skilled, but because he was heedless of his own or anyone else's safety. His carelessness once resulted in my having a broken leg. He was skating full out, oblivious to the havoc he caused, and he fell, swept my left leg as he fell, and my other leg snapped at the ankle causing a spiral fracture, the bone splintering in my skate with a sound like the popping of a champagne cork. I was sidelined for six weeks in a cast, and I spent the remainder of the season learning to walk again. I came back to play the following autumn, and when Neil continued to endanger me I said to him, "Neil, I'd appreciate it if you would stay away from me. I don't want you to break my leg again." To which he replied, "Did I get the puck? Because if I got the puck, then I don't care one way or another if I broke your leg or not. So, stop whining and fuck off!" I skated over to him, and said as firmly as I could, "Neil," meaning to add, "just play hockey and leave me alone," but I didn't get past the name when he head butted me, striking me full in the sternum and knocking me to the ice. I got back up on my feet and said to him, "Neil, you should be ashamed of yourself. You should go home and take your medication." He started to scream at me at the top of his lungs. I don't remember what he said, but the word "whining" kept burping out like a verbal eructation, a sort of angry belch. However, that was the last night he ever played hockey. I heard from his boss that the very next day he enrolled in anger management classes. I never saw him again.

My wife sometimes says to me, when I lament the behaviour of some of my fellow players, "John, it's a wonder you don't get beaten up more often." I've only been struck twice. I've only responded in kind once.

I say to myself, "John, just shut up and play." And sometimes, I manage to take my own council. Sometimes, I keep my mouth shut. When I said to one of the guys after a particularly nasty exchange, "Jamie, I've been wondering. What's it like being wrong about everything?"

"You should know," he said. And I take it to heart, "John, just shut up and play." And so, I do.

Goalies are different

The best goalie I ever had the pleasure of playing with is NHL superstar Dwayne Roloson who took the position between the pipes playing for us while he was still in high school. Every Wednesday he joined a group of men who called themselves 'the cardiac league'. We called ourselves that because our average age left us puffing on the bench between shifts with one worried eye of the defibrillator. Dwayne's mark of distinction was that he would not surrender the puck if he felt you weren't doing your job to defend him. He would guard his crease and send you away with a glare. Even though he was eighteen years my junior, he would rarely deign to give me the puck. I suppose he thought I just wasn't worthy of that generosity, even though I was on his defence and even though I was the first to arrive at his crease after he'd made an amazing save, this fifteen-year-old lad would send me on my way, puckless and chastened.

Over the years I've played with goalies that came to the net late in life, and goalies that have played that position since childhood. There's Doug who would go down in a sprawl to make a save, and then once he was down, he would need to turn himself around, grip the post, shimmy up onto his knees, grip the crossbar, pull himself erect, turn slowly, resume a defensive stance, while in the meantime, for fear of hurting him with a shot to the back of the head, or to the unprotected thigh or calf, we waited for him to complete this mock pole dance. That little drama took place every time he went down, and he went down every time someone shot the puck. We all liked him, but we didn't like playing against him because there was no challenge. And we didn't like protecting him because the questions "Did he shoot?" and "Did he score?" both have the same answer. If you shot the puck anywhere near the net, you scored. Eventually, Doug surrendered to bad health, went into hospital for an octuple bypass and did not return to play with us ever again.

I played with Jake, a frenetic farmer and a sometime visual artist who could be counted on to break a stick across the crossbar at least once every two games. Being what one might call a hot/cold goaltender, and easily agitated, he might abandon the team halfway through a game if he felt he wasn't playing well enough. In the dressing room, he fussed and fretted every time someone popped a cool beer. He threatened to report the guilty party to the arena staff. Not a popular goalie, he burned his bridges like the last sapper of a retreating army. There was madness in his method, and it was more madness than method. But in pickup, you need goalies and we'd put up with almost anything from a goalie.

And then there was Mike who does something of a striptease two or three times a game blaming equipment failure. We stand around, leaning against the boards, blowing our nails, passing the puck around a little, while Mike stops to adjust his straps. There's Al, the fastest dressing goalie in the world. He arrives last of all before the flood has ended, and in seconds he is fully suited up. I swear it's true. Like superman in a phone booth, or a werewolf in a mirror, or Dr. Jekyll becoming Mr. Hyde, he transforms himself before your very eyes, a mystical transfiguration. You look in his direction, and there he sits in street clothes. You look again, he's in his skivvies and then again and he's fully suited up in the time it takes you to tie a single skate he dons his goalie equipment. And then after the game is over, he's saying farewell as if he were dressed in tear-away pads. In all the years I played with Al, I never solved the mystery of his vestments. He seemed to fall into and out of his equipment with the ease that someone might dive into and emerge from a pool of water. In that sense he resembled Rusty and Ray who shared equipment and who rushed to and from the bench swapping gloves and sticks like two soldiers in the same foxhole with one rifle.

I played with goalies that would sweep opponents from the crease with the authority and vigor of the grim reaper. I played with goalies who were worse than sieves, they were colanders or bottomless buckets. I played with chatterboxes and men so quiet you wondered if they had language. One goalie almost always played best when he was drunk because he said a bottle of wine before the game helped him to take 'the edge off." I played with a goalie who is illiterate and a goalie that reads the classics. I played with a goalie we called Frying Pan Head because one time when he came into the dressing room sporting a sizeable goose egg on his boney forehead he told us his girlfriend had struck him with a frying pan. His theory for this violence on her part, "she was just testing me to see if I was a hitter." And he was proud of the fact that he didn't hit back. The next week he arrived with half his goalie equipment missing. "She threw it out the window," was his explanation for why he took to the ice without a blocker. He told us a story of how he'd followed a fellow CB radio user home and beaten the shit out of his truck with a baseball bat for an altercation they'd had over the wire. "I didn't know him, but I found out where he lived, and I taught his truck a lesson. I broke all the side mirrors and smashed the lights." I warned him that what he had done was a crime, and that he shouldn't be telling anyone this story because it was certain to get back to the victim and he might even be arrested and go to jail if he wasn't careful. He just grinned, hit his helmet hard with his stick and said, "When you get out on the ice, be sure to shoot it at my head. I like it best when you hit me in the head." That was Frying Pan who preferred to be called Super. He disappeared for several years after telling that story, and then one day when we were exchanging tales on the bench in the dressing room, I was regaling my fellow players with memories of this "real piece of work" we used to play with when a guy sitting there grinning to himself revealed his identity. "That's me you're talking about," he said. I looked closely at this grinning and rather plump fellow sitting there, and I realized it was *Frying*

Pan a.k.a. Super fifteen years older and forty pounds heavier. I thought to myself, 'me and my big fat mouth.' Everyone was laughing, including Frying Pan who instead of taking offence seemed to share in the delight of remembering the weird goalie with the proclivity for shouting 'shoot it at my head, shoot it at my head' when you skated in on him during practice. No longer a goalie, now a pudgy forward, he didn't mind being remembered as a piece of work. He seemed to love the notoriety. But I was mortified. A few of the guys who were there still tease me about the day we were telling stories and I told a tale that backfired.

These days I play in an over fifties league. The goalies change ends after a winning team scores five goals. Every time the goalies meet at centre ice, they pass and chat together for a few minutes. I've never managed to overhear what they talk about. This is goalie talk. It's private. Not to be shared. It is, I suspect, untranslatable. Like Basque, the language with no other common lingua franca, no shared roots, no sister tongue, this goalie talk, mystical babel with the power of supernatural sayings as it is when you might curse the goalie, by saying "shut out" thereby affecting the outcome of a nearly perfect game. This centre ice world where words have the power to make things happen. Where saying it is so, makes it so. Goalies are different, and if one asks the question, "Different from what?" The answer would be "Different from us, and even more so, different from themselves."

Away Games

Road trips were always a grand adventure. Sometimes-raucous good fun, sometimes disastrous mayhem, always fascinating experiences, they were loud-on-the-way, quiet-on-the-way home affairs involving much hard drinking, jolly good-natured jesting, and infrequently mean-spirited mayhem. The Skolars who were always good lads traveled in a reclaimed school bus used for transporting farm labour to and from the fields. Owned and operated by second-string goalie Russ 'Rusty' Sonnenberg, only he and Wayne 'Wacky' Wallace were licensed to drive. The bus we also called Rusty, was painted brown, and it did service over many trips to Blenheim a.k.a. 'paradise', the hometown of Ron 'Rocket' Richards, where we stayed at the local hotel making runs to Wheatley to play in the annual teacher's tournament. On a few of these excursions, I drove alone and stayed on my parents' farm near Highgate, only twenty kilometers east of paradise.

The Skolars were not the only team on which I played that took road trips. The 'Deaf Blind' team in Brantford decided to go on an excursion to the Aud in Buffalo to attend a game between the Sabers and the LA Kings to see Brantford hometown hero, hockey superstar Wayne Gretzky who played for the Kings at that time. We couldn't quite fill the roster so we encouraged Mike Vice to invite his rugby team along to help defer the cost of the rental of the bus. We stocked a cooler with seven cases of beer on ice, and met the bus at the local mall, arriving at 4 p.m. for a 4:30 departure time. However incredible it may seem, all the beer was gone before we left the parking lot. The rugby thugs descended upon the libation in the cooler like blowflies on a wildebeest. The highway entertainment involved lively singing of filthy rugby songs. One particular title I recall was a song called "The S & M Man." The rugby goons knew every word. We crossed the border without incident, and went our separate ways, but before the evening was over, two of the rugby lads were on their way to jail. In the middle of the game, one fellow caremed a beer glass off the head of a stranger's girlfriend. Another incident involved a guy attempting to disarm a police officer by unlatching the holster clip holding his gun in place. He made a racial epithet insulting the black officer's ethnic origins, and after a good drubbing was carted off to the Buffalo hoosegow for the night. On the way home, a few of the fellows who weren't sufficiently inebriated, managed to persuade the foolish driver to pull into an American 'Stop-and-Go' in order to buy munchies and, as if the legless fellows weren't drunk enough—more beer. The sensible few among us waited on the bus. Mike P. wanted some chips, so he went inside the establishment. A few minutes later, he came back looking rather grim bearing the news that we might be detained. "Those guys in there are going wild. They've eaten all the wieners in the hot dog display. They're popping the tabs on six packs of beer and guzzling them two at a time. They're ripping open bags of chips and are dumping them all over the floor. They're knocking over display cases and they're wrecking the place. They're refusing to pay for anything, and they're saying 'Only in America can we get away with this shit, man!' We're going to have to take up a collection, otherwise the clerk in there is going to call the police and we'll all be detained." Fortunately, things were sorted out. But if that weren't bad enough, someone lit a joint and our drunk and disorderly busload of mouthy yahoos stank of marijuana smoke as we headed for the border crossing. Oddly, we had no trouble getting back into Canada. The border guard seemed perfunctory and simply waved us through without incident. Feeling fortunate to get out of a foreign nation without further ado, Ian K. who had organized the trip said to me quietly, "I'm so sorry, John. We'll never invite these guys ever again. The next time we go on a road trip, we'll invite our wives and only a few of the guys, and we'll have a good time."

The following Friday, Randy G. was entertaining the dressing room regaling the guys who had not been on the Buffalo excursion with tales of how much fun we'd had. I'd had my fill of nonsense. I stood up, and told Randy to be quiet. "It wasn't fun." I said. "It was a disgrace. Everyone involved should be ashamed. How would you feel if you were that poor clerk working for a minimum wage while a bunch of hooligans ripped around your convenience store? I'm disgusted to be associated with you or with anyone who thinks that's funny. Ha, ha! We almost got arrested. Ha, ha! Someone threw a beer glass in the stands at the Aud and hit a woman in the back of the head. Funny!" Needless to say, I wasn't popular with the yahoos, but I think most everyone in the room agreed with me. What we'd been engaged in was shameful.

That occasion remains a nadir of my involvement with pickup hockey. Thankfully, it is also an exception. More often, the hijinks of traveling hockey teams are of a gentler humour. One of my favourite pranks involved the time when the Skolars were on their way to Blenheim. There had been much drinking, and we'd pulled over to the side of the road to relieve ourselves. We gathered shoulder to shoulder with our backs to the ditch facing the slab-sided bus, pulling down our trouser flies and letting loose with yellow arcs of urine. Darcy 'Dead-Eye' Douglas having finished his own business quick, ran to the bus, hopped into the driver's seat, put the bus in gear and drove fifty yards down the road leaving twenty guys, their Johnsons exposed to the street, skate laces of urine hissing in the gravel, guys twisting and turning, inadvertently drenching each other's pant legs, staining the cloth to the knee in a frantic effort to button up and be done. Everyone was laughing and lovingly cursing Dead-Eye who could always be counted on for an amusing caper.

Another team I played for, Wes Stewart's group out of Harley, decided we would sign up to play in the Plattsville tournament. We were a motley crew of ad hoc players comprised of a select group of Wes's family cobbled together with enough guys to ice a team. Fortunately, for the most part, we didn't care to win; we only cared to play. We lost our first game thirteen to zero to a team that was so grateful. "This is the first time we've ever won a game in a tournament," one particularly appreciative fellow said by way of congratulating us during the handshake at the end of the game. "We've been enrolled every year for the last ten years running and we haven't won a game until now. Thanks, fellas." A disgruntled defenseman grumbled in the dressing room about our performance in general and his fellow defensemen in particular. Wes and I being the other two defensemen, "Let's keep track of plus minus then, if you're so good," I challenged. And so, I did. I kept track. We lost the next game fifteen to two, and Wes and my plus minus was plus two. That meant his plus minus was minus fifteen. You would have thought that would shut him up. It did not. But then he's a fellow with a criminal record for kiting cheques, so why should anyone care what he thinks.

On the way home from our away games in Wheatley, the bus was usually quiet, the air noisome and brumous and thick with the sickening aftertaste of effulgent bloody Caesar flatulence, men obstreperous and groggy with hangover headaches, and much rummy stentorian post Captain Morgan snoring. Woody's jaw already sore from laughter, Rocket might say, "Are we havin' some fun now, boys?" The hawks and the sparrows all groaning from indulgence might smile weakly and sing a feeble chorus of Willy Nelson's "On the Road Again," as they fall into a post-traumatic stupor, catching a few well-earned winks to freshen themselves for the future.

Injuries

Over the years I've seen some pretty serious injuries. Mostly due to unintentional contact, and sometimes involving no one but the injured party, I've seen a few fellows carried off in stretchers, and a few green in the gills in the dressing room. The worst of these mishaps occurred the day Dean turned forty. He was just celebrating an unusual occurrence. He'd scored a goal. Skating a little too hard, he'd lost his footing a few metres from the corner and slammed skate blade first into the boards, thus shattering his ankle, driving his talus two inches into his splintering tibia thereby shortening himself by two inches on one leg. We didn't know how bad it was at the time, but he was still hallucinating from the pain a few hours later in the emergency room waiting for the arrival of the surgeon. Luckily no one had bothered to loosen or remove his skate boot before the ambulance came. That would have been a disaster, the surgeon told his agitated wife. When I went to see Dean in hospital after the game, I witnessed him writhing in pain despite a heavy dose of morphine, his ankle wrapped in an ice pack, blue to the knee, and he was screaming so loud you could almost hear him from the parking lot. I'm still ginger about going into the corners or skating hard with someone inclined to be careless near the boards.

The night my own leg was broken, I suffered a spiral fracture in the bone just above the ankle. It felt like a champagne cork going off in my skate. I limped to the bench, removed my skate, walked a few steps, put my skate back on, went out on the next shift thinking "surely if it were broken I'd feel far worse than I do …" I skated down the ice, chasing the fellow with the puck, he swerved, I swerved and I almost blacked out from the pain. "Okay," I thought. This can't be good. I skated off the ice, went to the dressing room, changed into my street clothes, drove home, limped up the stairs, put on my pajamas, crawled into bed, turned over, winced once, whimpered, trying not to disturb my wife, who woke up, turned on the light, and said, "What's going on?" Not wanting to make a fuss, I said, "I think I might have broken my leg. I'm not sure, though." "Get up, and get to the hospital," Cathy said. She's a no nonsense girl, and I'm an uxorious husband. I got up, dressed in the dark, limped the two long blocks to the hospital, and went to emergency, which wasn't too busy since it was around 2:30 a.m. by the time I'd arrived. "I think I might have broken my leg," I said to the on-call doctor. "Oh, you've broken your leg, alright." He replied when I'd suggested I might be wrong. An hour later, I crutched my way home, my shin limed to the knee, arriving in time to catch a couple of hours sleep before dawn. Unfortunately, we'd booked a vacation in Florida and we were due to drive south the very next week in our stick-shift jeep. We rented a van, invited my brother-in-law and his children to accompany us provided he was able to drive. We had a wonderful fun-in-the sun vacation in Florida. Six weeks later, after the removal of the cast, I had to learn to walk again. The hockey season ended early for me that year.

I saw a guy split his face open from his upper lip along the philtrum to the base of his nose, liberating two front teeth in the process. He'd been playing rough and checking hard and close when he went down in such a way that the heel of a skate blade struck him like an axe blow to the incisors. Everyone knew it was his own fault. That said, the fellow whose skate he bit felt bad about it.

Another occasion, Sully was skating hard down the ice when he suddenly went down. He yelped, "Who the fuck did that?" We'd all seen him fall, and everyone knew it was bad. But we also knew that he went down all by himself. No one had done anything wrong. His hamstring had snapped like an over-tightened piano wire. His flesh went from being in the full-pinkish flush of good health to being bleached with white splotches to being greenish-grey in a matter of seconds. He was clearly in agony. The game was over in that instant. We dare not move him. A farmer with horses to tend and heifers to fatten at home, we knew we wouldn't see him again for a while. He still hasn't returned to the fold. We had the end of year party at his house that summer, and his prognosis remains rather bleak.

These injuries are few and far between. As I age, career-enders occur more often than they used to, sometimes more often than they should. When a guy goes down after sixty, it takes him a lot longer to get back up. According to one of the wives making an observation at a hockey banquet, "It's hard to believe these guys are over sixty and some over seventy. They all look so young and healthy." That said, I'm the delicate kind. I'd rather lose the puck than the ability to play the next game. I've seen too many accidents. This past Christmas, I woke in the morning with septic bursitis. I'd taken a puck in the knee. It had wormed under my pad and struck me hard on exposed bone. It sidelined me for three games. Once I was made of iron. Now I'm a breakable man.

Blood on the ice, eyes fluttering from a blow to the head, flesh gone green from a heart attack, no one wants to see these, but I've seen them. They're all consequences of being in the game when the game turns against you. Now I've entered the phase when the talk in the dressing room involves conversations about successful hernia operations, knee and hip replacements, open-heart and bypass surgery, gall bladder attacks, bouts of pneumonia, swollen prostates, kidney stones, deep bruises, cancer of the lip, pulled groins, arthritic joints, and playing through the pain. It's the unnecessary injuries I want to avoid.

The vocabulary of water

We live on the shore of Lake Erie. Early rising rewards the insomniac with red dawn blushing over blue water. Late afternoons in winter and ten o'clock evenings in summer the daylight fades to crimson and my wife and I will sit transfixed by sunfire. On dark clear nights we witness the lights of Erie, Pennsylvania glowing on the horizon from the forty-mile-away American shores. My friend, the late poet Margaret Avison, wrote to me in her last correspondence lamenting her lameness and near blindness, "At least I still have my daily skies." And so, wisdom remains grateful for the perceived beauty of small blessings. "No one stuffs the world in at your eyes," she had cautioned in an early sonnet.

I recently witnessed the upside-down flight of two Canada geese flying topsy-turvy in a chevron coming in for a landing on the lake. I discovered that this method of slowing their flight is quite common amongst waterfowl and the word for it is *whiffling*. When I mentioned this phenomenon to my fellow hockey players in a free wheeling conversation had on the hockey bench while we were dressing for the game, someone said, "Isn't it interesting. Who would have thought we'd be talking of such things in a hockey dressing room." To this I said, "I'm interested in everything, except for the lumber business." When Bill Dunkley challenged that by saying, "Why not the lumber business, John?" "Well," said I, "When I used to work unloading train cars for the lumber yard, every once in a while I got a little board." At that a much deserved groaning grumbled round the dressing room like fart smell.

Last winter on the lake was a good one. The entire surface of the bay froze over and the smooth ice near shore was cleared of snow and kept groomed by a local restaurateur with an establishment on the beach and a truck with a fixed blade. He cleaned and kept clean a rink-sized pad on which he set two hockey nets for all comers. On Christmas morning my Thai daughter-in-law Bo donned her brand new skates and for the first time since coming to Canada and partook in the Canadian tradition of an outdoor skate. She, my son, our Jack Russell pup Sarge and I joined a half-a-dozen other enthusiasts chasing joy in a chill wind on a brilliant winter morning. Sarge, being a fanatic digger, spent most of his time scrabbling shine on a single slippery spot, clawing away at the frozen surface as if he meant to rescue someone buried alive in the ice. Yes indeed, 2011 was a good year for lake ice. It came early and stayed late, providing months of winter pleasure.

However, this past winter has been completely different. Too warm for a deep freeze, it has been a season of erratic and unreliable temperatures rarely dipping below 0 degrees. And yet there has been much to delight those of us addicted to paying attention to the ever-changing beauty of an ever-changing world. And so, I've made something of a study of the varieties of ice this year. The range of freeze and thaw and the long list and copious vocabulary of water has been of profound interest. If Margaret had her daily skies to celebrate, I've had my daily varieties of ice. I've always loved minutiae and the rewarding particulars of learning. From reading author Bill Bryson I learned that the amount of water within the atmosphere, in the sky, and both on the surface and beneath the surface of the earth remains constant. By reading a 2002 newspaper article on global warming I learned of the Larsen B ice shelf that broke away from Antarctica now free floating as it rots in the open waters of the ocean, that in the melting ice of that shelf there is enough water to feed the Nile River for one hundred years. From reading the findings of geologists I learned that levels in the Great Lakes are far more dependent upon aquifers than annual rainfall. By listening to friend Roger Bell I was reminded of the prodigious evaporation that occurs during mild winters when open water fails to freeze. And from studying research on the physics of freezing I learned that the deeper you go, the colder the water, and that water freezes in the depths first and then the buoyant solids float to the surface and fuse there according to the conditions they find on top.

2012 has been a mild winter in southwestern Ontario, though not without a sufficiency of colder days to provide the observer with varieties of ice that give rise to the need for an extensive lexicon necessary for precision of description. From the first cold days of December through to the last cold days of March we have had a plethora of formations, enough to challenge the vocabulary of even the most erudite glaciologist.

In February, near Valentine's, the most common formation to be seen was pancake ice. This predominantly circular ice with a raised rim crowded the local shores in grey-white swells, floating there in the thousands like drab water lilies undulating on the waves. Earlier in the season there was a sufficiency of slush and grease ice washing ashore and accumulating in filthy hills crowning the sand along the breakwalls making surefooted walking nearly impossible. I made the mistake of testing the lumps and mounds and heaps and berms and found myself thigh deep in the slushy sponge. Some days the harbour would reward the silence with the glass-on-glass drag-sound of windowpanes of sheet ice grinding together along crack lines or forming half-broken acres of raft ice. My favourite of all formations was the frazil ice with fine spicules of sharp shards piercing the surface suspended in the water like vandalism in the glass factory. One winter a few years ago, the ice blew in jamming the harbour forming great hills and sharp ridges far enough off shore to tantalize the tourists. Hundreds of visitors braved the distance and climbed the sastruga looming on the edge of open regions under dark and ominous shadows of water sky. The local paper printed a photograph of these foolish tourists and warning them to heed the experience of the locals said, "What you're doing is not safe."

    I've trekked the arctic and seen blue ice older than time. I've walked on the Penny Glacier and slaked my thirst in the glacial melt of the Weasel River. Once I fell through a crack in stranded ice and found myself deposited ten feet below on the gravely shore of a fjord. I walked in the shadow of bummock and climbed the crackling firn. Though where I live I love the winter best when it presents the gift of reliable ice, this winter has been its own unending delight for the poet in me who loves the words even more than the things that they describe. So the whiffling goose might flip and thrust his flying feet in the air to amaze and delight, but it's the word whiffling that gives the action its deeper thrill. My very mind itself is whiffling within me as I write.

Remembering Ice

I'm thinking now of the fragrance of ice. How it sometimes lifts from the surface of the world with the cold-rich aroma of wool and wet dust. Pure water is a bland, odourless, lakeless, and infragrant liquid with little to recommend itself to the nose. But water-into-ice is rarely as pure as Eden's elixir Adam's ale. Arena surface made from town water smells of the taste of fluoridation and the cleansing chemical corruption that comes with overuse. The snow heaped by the door stinks of the pong of road salt blended with earth-brown lane gravel and the lingering perfume of much-used motor oil scraped from rainbows that glowed with a weird and lovely incandescence. Those mounds are blackened and marbled through with the stinking detritus of half-eaten school lunches, banana peels, apple cores, chocolate bar wrappers and cigarettes butts. But natural ice, the smooth-as-glass skaters' paradise where sharp blades cut into the surface with a scarring perfection like a glass-cutter's knife etching into a window pane, gives off the full-breath perfume of Canadian winter with that deeply satisfying hollow sound heard like the click of a fingernail on the glaze of a swimmer's mask. It is in and of the world that we are then. Taking in the resin-aromas of the near-at-hand snow-laden pine, the livid redness of the dogwood whippets, the prickly burdock badging our scarves and coat hems, with new snow on the wind like flights of milkweed down and the loud chorus of song sparrows thrilling the hedges.

Counting the loss...

> *"He stepped onto the ice circled twice fell flat and died."*
> Dying on the Ice at 39 is Hard
> — John B. Lee

Although I've never witnessed death on the ice, I've certainly experienced its aftermath. On at least four occasions I've arrived at an arena to play hockey only moments after someone has died instantly. The person in question has always been thirty-nine years of age. In most cases the victim perished during warm ups. Once at a hockey tournament in Wheatley, we arrived at the rink just as the ambulance attendants were carrying a body from the surface of the ice. The entire atmosphere of the building was heavy with grief and abuzz with talk concerning what had occurred. A team from Toronto had just begun to skate in advance of the game when one of their teammates fell flat out and remained there unmoving. When the doctor arrived at his side, he was heard to pronounce that he must have died instantly. "Dead before he hit the ice," was how he'd put it. "There was never any hope."

We all felt sorry for his teammates. We talked for a while in hushed tones about how sad the news would be for his friends and we gave our condolences to strangers on their way as they were with their sorrowful burden.

I experienced similar deaths over the course of the next several hockey seasons. Twice in Paris, just as I arrived to suit up for the game we played every Tuesday night, taking to the ice at an uncivilized hour, from 10:30-11:30, I heard news of a very comparable nature, "Did you hear what happened? A guy died just before we got here. He was in good shape, young I think; I heard he was only thirty-nine. Seems he just stepped on the ice, skated around a couple of times, and fell down dead. Dead before he hit the ice. That's what I heard. Didn't you see the ambulance? I'm surprised you didn't meet the paramedics in the parking lot." This same story repeated itself on two subsequent occasions. Once again in Paris, and once when I was playing in St. George.

I wrote a poem about the Wheatley tragedy and I won the 1989 Nova Scotia Poetry Award for that poem. When I read the poem at the ceremony celebrating my win in Halifax, there was a woman in attendance there who stood up in the middle of my reading, barely able to control her emotions, and made a very discrete and dignified exit from the room. She spoke with me afterwards saying, "I hope you don't think I took offense at your poem. The little I heard of it was wonderful, but you have to understand, I just lost my husband who died on the ice exactly as you described. And coincidentally, he had just celebrated his thirty-ninth birthday. Your poem hit too close to home."

She and I got chatting about the number of people we knew who'd died on the ice. I told her about my friend Scott who'd had an English teacher who'd died suddenly while playing hockey. "You know," she said, "I read somewhere that this sudden death syndrome in hockey players has something to do with the exhaust fumes that hover in the stale arena air after the machine has cleaned the ice. It has something to do with carbon monoxide levels, poor ventilation in the rink, and the badly filtered exhaust from the engine."

I don't know whether she's correct, but in my experience, all the sudden deaths I know of occurred either during the warm-ups or in the first few minutes of play. A combination of an undiagnosed heart ailment, the air quality in the arena, and the deep breaths taken by players during the exertions at the start of a warm up gives credence to this anecdotal theory. Now it is very common for hockey arenas to have defibrillators in the building to deal with the frequency of an urgent need to shock the heart alive. Perhaps that's why they now have these life-saving devices in almost every arena in Ontario.

Not every loss I've experienced has occurred on the ice. I've recently attended the funerals of two close friends who played with my first team, *The Skatin' Skolars*. A few years ago, I received a call on Christmas day from a colleague phoning to tell me that our pal Ralph Evans had died that day. A very athletic man and an extremely popular and well-liked fellow, Ralph 'Elbows' Evans had been skiing in the morning, and was dead by dusk. Although the reason for his passing remains something of a mystery, the most persuasive diagnosis suggests that he had somehow contracted clostridium. Whatever the case, after a brisk morning ski, Ralph came down with a fever. By mid-afternoon, the fever was raging and his temperature was so high that the nurses thrust his fiery body into an ice bath. Even that failed to bring the fever under control. By nightfall he had passed away.

The entire hockey team donned their team sweaters for the funeral service. The poll bearers likewise wore their jerseys as they carried the casket to the hearse for its final resting place. We took Ralph's loss hard. He was indeed much loved. We all dabbed our eyes to remember our fallen pal. All who knew him will miss Ralph "Elbows" Evans.

Only a short time later we buried another teammate. Ray Antoniolli had been one of our goalies. An engaging, hard-drinking Italian farm lad, Ray was loved by all who knew him. When he played net, he used to jest about having to have a glass of wine or two to, as he put it, "get the edge off," so he could steady his nerves and quicken his hands. A few years back, he'd started to notice that his hands and feet were getting cold. He tried wearing wool gloves inside his hockey gloves to no avail. He went to the doctor and was diagnosed as suffering from scleroderma, an autoimmune disease associated with hardening of the flesh. Though Ray quit playing net, he continued to come to the games and was always a happy addition to any team activity. Ray was always good for a laugh. Once he borrowed his wife's bikini, entered a local bathing beauty contest and won. At his surprise sixtieth birthday party, he walked into the Waterford Legion accompanied by his wife, Mary, took one look at the crowd of well-wishers gathered there, laughed, said "you bastards" and poured the entire contents of a full bottle of beer over his own head. The year before he died, although he was feeling quite poorly, he drove his vintage tractor in the Norfolk

Heritage Tractor Drive beginning in Waterford and ending in Jarvis by way of Hagersville. Although Ray suffered terrible pain at the end of his life, he remained positive and spirited and will be fondly remembered by all who knew him.

He once said of me, "Do you mind if I drink from John's glass. I want to find out if I drink what he's drinking if I'll know everything too." I laughed when I heard that. Ray was incapable of being cruel. He said it in good fun, and I know he meant it as a gentle jest for a fellow player who sometimes seems just a little too full of himself to be one of the guys. I'd gladly take a humble sip from Ray's glass any day. Everyone who knew him loved him and I remember him fondly as a good man who died before his time.

I've also experienced the loss of a few men I didn't know too well. One summer, we picked up a new goalie. We were always looking for reliable goalies in pickup hockey. The only things that mattered were that they had goalie equipment, and that they arrive on time so that they'd be first on the ice and last to leave. In the nineties, we managed to get a guy to play who agreed to come out as long as he could bring his thirteen-year-old son. We agreed and he joined us along with his lad. His name was George Smart, and his son Daryl was a pretty good hockey player for such a young fellow, and he didn't mind playing with a bunch of washed up old guys. We called ourselves "the cardiac league' and we played Wednesday nights in the summer in Simcoe at the Fairgrounds arena. The ice was always chalky, and our equipment sometimes chafed our sunburns at the strap lines, but we didn't mind that. We loved the game even on a hot July evening or a torpid August dusk. When George first started coming out, he had just gotten his pilot's license and was looking forward to his inaugural solo flight in his homemade one-man airplane. I remember him talking excitedly in anticipation of his plans. I imagined him as a fledgling leaping the rim of the nest and soaring into the blue. He described his plane as resembling the early experimental prototypes flown by Orville Wright, sort of a bicycle in the sky. All his life he'd dreamed of owning and flying his own plane and he built in his garage.

The following week, I sat on the bench in the dressing room. A guy sat down next to me and said, "Did you hear what happened to George? He crashed his plane and died. He just went up in the air, stalled out, and dropped out of the sky like a shot duck. He drilled that homemade plane right into the ground at the airport in Brantford. Poor fellow. I feel so sorry for his son."

I'd read the story in the newspaper, but I hadn't made the connection. I played hockey with guys who flew out of the Brantford airport. One of them owned an airplane repair business. I'd actually talked with him about the tragedy. Thinking the victim had been a stranger, I'd inquired as to what Bud had thought of the whole affair. "Those homemade planes are death traps. They should be made illegal. They're unforgiving things. There's not a chance in hell to survive; if they stall out, you're done. You certainly can't bring them in for a safe landing. The poor bugger. I saw it happen. He was so happy. I certainly wouldn't ever fly one of those contraptions. Sad way to die. But I guess he died doing something he loved."

Ironically, Bud, a very experienced pilot, had lost his own brother only a few years before in a tragic plane crash in Lake Erie. Terry was a very experienced pilot as well. He'd suffered the tragic loss of his wife only a very short while after I'd met him. In 1984 my wife and I moved to Brantford. The real estate agent who'd sold us our house played pickup hockey in Paris. His best friend worked for us renovating our house on Palmerston Avenue in the city. Both of them asked me if I wanted to join them on Tuesday nights at Syl Apps arena where a great group of guys played for an hour late in the evening. They were a pretty motley crew. One guy played in dress pants with almost no equipment. Another fellow wore blue sweat pants bulging over his shin pads like the warting of poorly leavened bread. Some of them mistook me for a real hockey player because I had every piece of equipment worn by true athletes. I soon disabused them of this misconception when we started to play. The quality of play ranged from guys who could barely skate to guys with soft hands and quick reflexes. None of us were what you might call talented, but some were young enough to be fast and dumb enough to be confident. The guy who organized this group was a fun-loving very likeable fellow named Terry Field.

Terry was a forty-something blond-haired friendly sort of guy with much hail-fellow well-met charm. He loved to josh and joke and keep us entertained with light-hearted talk. I liked him immediately and admired his easy ways. Shortly after I started playing with this group of guys, Terry's wife took sick and was diagnosed with a very virulent form of cancer. The cancer galloped and she died quite quickly. Terry was clearly heartbroken by his loss. We consoled him for a while, but he made it clear that although he felt the loss quite deeply, he'd rather just play hockey and not talk about it. Then he met a woman and fell in love. "I'd thought that part of my life was done when my wife died." He'd said to us. "But I found love again." And we were very happy for him.

One fateful night in the summer of 1986, he and his bride-to-be vanished over Lake Erie. I heard from his brother Bud that he'd been in Cleveland with his fiancé, that he'd told the local air-traffic controllers that it looked like it might storm so he set out immediately for home, flying his Cessna over the lake heading for the Brantford airport. Brother Bud, refusing to believe the worst, kept up a vigilant campaign in search of his brother. His father told a reporter, "We just stand right here and hope somebody will call and tell us what's happening. We can always hope for the best. I'm kind of expecting him to walk through the door. He's always flying off somewhere."

Eventually, after finding a few scraps, a floating cushion, a baseball cap, the family held a memorial service at the United Church in Paris. I joined the crowd of mourners there where Bud's wife, Jane, delivered a profoundly moving eulogy. With an unquavering voice she celebrated the life of Terry and his intended. From then on, Bud took over running the hockey. I never forgot the dignity with which the Field family suffered the loss of their dear brother Terry. When I recently mentioned this tragedy to a friend with whom I play hockey now, a guy by the name of Mike Fletcher, he immediately remembered the affair. Mike is a professional deep-sea diver, and at the time of the accident Bud had called him requesting that he take part in the search for the lost plane. We spoke in reverent terms about the crash. Mike told me that it had been established that the Cessna had flown into an intense thunderstorm shortly after taking off. One eyewitness heard a plane engine from the vantage of a boat on the lake. According to that individual it sounded like the plane was in distress. The engine seemed to choke out and stall. It's believed that the small plane simply broke up in the turbulence and crashed. Perhaps it was struck by lightning since aviation weather observers had counted more than a dozen lightning bolts during a ten-minute period in the area where the Cessna was last reported. After Bud contacted Mike in an effort to persuade him to join in the search for the plane, Mike viewed the details and informed Bud that it was highly unlikely that they would find anything.

    The day that Mike and I talked about this plane crash, Mike offered to give me his notes on the story. "If you write about this, make sure you do so in a dignified way. I'd hate to think that you might write something that would insult the family." The same day, over a beer at the local pub in Port Dover, Mike regaled us with a story about a guy named Billy Smith. A local smuggler of some fame not to be confused with the NHL hockey goalie Billy Smith—"Not that Billy Smith," Mike Fletcher had said to another guy at our table who'd joked, "Didn't he used to play hockey for the New York Islanders?" When I got home that day, my son Sean had left an email message on my computer asking me, "Dad, have you ever heard of a hockey goalie named Billy Smith? I played an exhibition game with him today. I got you an autographed photo. I hope you'll like it." I could not help but be struck by the coincidence. It seems the idea of six degrees of separation is an understatement.

    To this day, I feel the loss of Terry Field, Ralph Evans, Ray Antoniolli, and even George Smart whom I barely knew. I need only close my eyes to see the mischief in their smiling faces. George's gleeful anticipation of a first flight, Terry's tragic disappearance after having logged nearly ten thousand hours in the air, Ralph's sudden passing and Ray's slow decline, but beneath this and behind it all, lie fond memories of the time we shared playing the game we love. Life's far too short to focus on the loss. I think on what I've gained by having known these fellows. And I only hope, that I've managed to honour them just a little, remembering them fondly, celebrating a shared joy for those moments we spent together on the ice and off. One might say to the spirit of these lost friends, "Keep your head up," and in so saying, glimpse the ghost of a smile, the last thing to vanish from the mind remembering these good men.

Counting the Loss ii

The day Jamie came to tell me he was dying, he also gave me the gift of the word clapperdudgeon. Bookish like me, he knew I'd love this new word. "A clapperdudgeon is a beggar who pales the flesh with arsenic in order to excite a deeper sympathy for his plight," he said, adding, "often they're children." And then he told me his gall bladder was sludgy with stones and having gone to the doctor with that small complaint he'd been diagnosed with terminal cancer. "I've been given three years, provided I submit to chemotherapy. I want to play hockey again. I know you still play Wednesday nights. Maybe you might pick me up on the way and we'll have a good time." Every Monday he submitted to chemo, and then on Wednesday night he skated. Obviously drained by the toxins he was ingesting, he barely made it through the scrimmage and looking rather grey he often sat puffing on the bench waving off his next shift.

Jamie lived in a beam and dowel house he'd built himself straddling the beams and hammering home the dowels without using a single nail. He and his wife, their two children, a big slobber-tongued dog Biko, named for the South African martyred opponent of Apartheid, and several cats lived on a large acreage a few kilometers outside of the city of Brantford where he'd once owned a book store. He'd gone out of business a few years before and now he was operating a book-order business out of his house. Originally from Montreal, he'd established himself in the city once described by the mayor as having "the ugliest main street in all of Canada." I remembered Brantford from my childhood when I'd read an article listing "the best and worst" things in our nation. That piece appeared in the weekend insert in the *London Free Press*. For whatever reason, I have a clear recollection of the fact that Brantford was sited as the place where one might find the best French fries and the worst drinking water in the nation. At the time I had no idea where Brantford was. My university roommate hailed from Brantford. And then, in 1984 my wife, our two sons and I moved to the city where we would live for the next twenty years. I met Jamie when I visited his bookstore. We became instant friends. I brought him to play hockey in Paris on Tuesday nights. Then he joined me on Wednesdays in Simcoe. He quit hockey for a while when he was building his house. He lost his business due to the downturn in the economy. And then, after he started a book order business out of his house, I phoned him up and ordered a copy of Australian poet Les Murray's selected poems.

The day he came to my house to deliver the book, he also delivered the bad news concerning his own failing health, and the gift of that lovely little word, *clapperdudgeon*. After a few months of chemo, the doctors told him he was cancer free. A year passed, and my phone rang. It was Jamie, and he was in hospital. I went to see him and he told me through the tears that he was dying. "I have two years to live," he'd said. "I'm not afraid to die. I'm just disappointed not to have made more of a difference in the world. I'm grieving because my children aren't yet grown, and I feel like I've failed them." Jamie had been a committed pacifist and a dedicated environmentalist. My wife and I had both voted for him when he ran as the candidate for the local Green Party. We'd often talked long into the night lamenting the violence in the world. When he'd taken a job driving taxi, he told me it was all he could do to maintain his sympathy for the poor. "When the welfare cheques came, they'd call for a cab and I'd pick up a hot breakfast and drive it across the city. By the time I got there the food was cold. What a waste of money! It was all I could do not to hate them." He listened to Yo Yo Ma's recordings of Bach's cello suites, read Giovanni Vico, debated the merits of the denial of desire, wrote philosophical dithyrambs in the night, and died two days after my first last and only visit to see him in hospital. The phone rang, his wife said to me, "John, Jamie's gone. He died in my arms." And she wept.

I saw Val in the airport lounge three years later. I was on my way to Paris, France and she was leaving on a flight to Chicago to visit her daughter who had accepted a position in the history department at the University of Chicago. A brilliant student, she had articled at Cambridge and been snapped up as something of an academic wonder. Val introduced me to her second husband saying of me, "This is John. He was Jamie's best friend."

When I think of Jamie now, I remember the night we took our young sons with us to watch us play hockey. Jamie and I were on the ice, and when we looked up we saw our lads hanging from the railing on the second level of the arena, dangling there like two monkeys their fingers gripping the metal suspended fifteen feet above an unforgiving cement floor. Screaming simultaneously, I shouted "Sean!" and Jamie shouted "Brandon!" That was the last time we ever allowed our sons to accompany us to the rink while we played. We loved our wild lads, but we didn't trust them to sit quietly. They were always up to something. I also smile to remember the one occasion when Jamie and I were stopping for snacks on the way home and we both clapped eyes on the *National Enquirer*. On the cover there was a photograph of a submarine surfacing from the water with a rather swarthy looking figure emerging from the conning tower. The caption read, "Iraqi sub spotted in Lake Michigan." I laughed and said, "I suppose it must have come spawning up Niagara Falls like a salmon." "Perhaps they choppered it in and dropped it from the sky." Jamie countered. "Imagine the lock pilot steering it through the Welland Canal and wondering at the strange silence of the crew." "Perhaps it was introduced as a foreign species, like Rainbow smelt at Chrystal Lake in 1912." My son Sean, having taken up hockey on Wednesday nights, was there as well, and we all laughed looking at that doctored photograph and wondering about a world where credulous people were duped by conspicuously silly nonsense. My son remembered Jamie eating a big bag of seasoned pork rinds and drinking a forty-ounce bottle of Coca-Cola on the way home from hockey. "That can't be good for you," he added.

I think of Jamie often and always fondly. After all, as his widow said, I was his best friend. I wrote a poem about that day, the day he visited with the sad news of his failing health.

Tripped by Andy Bathgate

Since birth, my life has been strangely connected to that of New York Rangers' hockey superstar Andy Bathgate. He doesn't know it, but I do. At six years of age, I donned my first hockey uniform. I wore a wool sweater emblazoned by the Rangers logo. I wore Rangers socks and a Rangers toque. My father insisted on that. My mother told me recently that particular uniform was the only thing he absolutely demanded.

Like most Canadian boys of my generation, I sent away for and received a series of Bee Hive Hockey Cards mailed to me by Saint Lawrence Starch Company. I think they were random selections. I didn't know it then, but I had acquired a few of the best players who ever played professional hockey. I had Maurice Rocket Richard, Gordy Howe, Boom Boom Geoffrion, Bobby Hull, Red Kelly, Tim Horton, Frank Mahovlich, and Andy Bathgate. As a preteen, although I loved hockey culture, I'm not sure I knew exactly who Andy Bathgate was.

When it was time to favour my own team, I chose the Chicago Black Hawks. Most of my childhood friends were fans of either the Toronto Maple Leafs or Detroit Red Wings. I grew up in Kent County and Detroit was our closest big city. Every September, we traveled to Detroit, crossing the border to purchase new clothes and school supplies. But I didn't like the Wings and I didn't admire Gordy Howe. He was too rough for my taste. As a red-blooded Canadian lad, I should have been either a Habs or a Leaf fan. But from the original six, I chose the Chicago logo, often described to be the best logo in all of professional sports. I thrilled to the talents of superstar Bobby Hull a.k.a, the Golden Jet. I liked the word Chicago. Drawn to the mystique of the windy city perhaps because my paternal grandfather had shown at the International Livestock Exposition for forty years or perhaps because of my father's lifelong fascination with organized crime. To this day, I wear a Black Hawks sweater when I take to the ice.

Then one fateful night in the winter of 1979 when *The Skatin' Skolars* took on the NHL Old-Timers and staged an exhibition game to raise funds for the local minor hockey league, I came into close contact with a few of the famous retirees. I recognized the names of a few of the players we played against that evening. There was Norm Ullman, Ron Ellis, Wilf Paiement and Andy Bathgate. I was on the ice, away from the play, waiting for something happen, when standing shoulder to shoulder with Andy Bathgate, he slipped the blade of his stick into the slot of my skates, gave a slight pull sending me sprawling at his feet. He looked down. I looked up. He gave a big shit-eating grin, and said in a soft voice, "Keep your head up, kid," and skated away. That relatively inconsequential exchange between Andy Bathgate and me remains something of an apotheosis of my hapless hockey career. The ref didn't see a thing. I picked myself up, dusted myself off, and went on with the game of a lifetime.

I didn't put two and two together until this past spring when my first cousin Susan Scaman née McNaughton mentioned that her Uncle Ronnie had been Andy Bathgate's best friend. He and Andy and their wives holidayed together and played golf together until Ronnie passed away in the winter of 2011. When her Uncle Ronnie died, Andy Bathgate had delivered the eulogy at his funeral. Ronnie had owned and operated a convenience store across the street from the Guelph arena. "That was probably when they met," Susan said. While Andy played for Guelph, the McNaughton brothers Ronnie and Billy attended every game.

"When my Grandmother McNaughton passed away, I was

sixteen," cousin Susan told me, "and I attended the funeral without my Mother. Family all went back to Uncle Ronnie's for coffee after the service. My cousin Bill, who was about twelve at the time, a true hockey player through his younger years, said to me—'there's Andy Bathgate over there.' I asked, 'Who's Andy Bathgate?' I'm sure he thought I was a pretty dumb girl, but coming from a family that didn't play hockey except on the front pond, I had no idea who this famous NHL player was. I just remember him being very good looking and a true gentleman."

So, even though Andy Bathgate doesn't know me, and he probably wouldn't remember the night he tripped me in the big game, I know him. I wore his sweater when I was six. My father insisted on that. And now I know why my father smiled so broadly when I told him, "Dad, I was tripped by Andy Bathgate."

The swear jar—words with the flavour of soap

I play hockey with a guy who uses the 'f' word so often in conversation that when he talks in the dressing room he could fill a swear jar in the time it would take a bar maid to draw a single glass of your favourite draft to the foam line. I'm sure *The Skatin' Skolars* would be surprised to hear this, but when my friend Gary came to play with the Skolars he was most taken aback by what he described as the poverty of their language. "I would not have believed teachers capable of using the 'f' word so freely. In fact I find it hard to believe they're schoolteachers," he told me recently when I reminded him of the fact that he had played with us once long ago.

I would be lying if I were to say that I do not swear. However, for the most part, I swear only on the ice, and then only when I'm exasperated by my own ineptitude. Cursing myself for incompetence with the puck, I have been the recipient of 'the most dramatic player award' several years running. If you can envision Groucho Marx doing his hidee ho dance in *Duck Soup*, add to that a soupcon of profanity by someone in full hockey gear wielding his stick like a mad lancer doing a tap routine on ice skates, then you have a reliable image of my style. I have my own particular flagless semaphore. I prize a different signal for every imagined infraction. And though I swear like a carpenter striking his thumb, I'm absolutely decorous in the dressing room or in conversation over wings and beer in the bar after the game.

When I was a boy, I knew the flavour of vulgarity. It tasted of the perfumed blend of lilac and lye. Profanity foamed on my tongue like madness in a dog. I rarely heard my farmer father swear, and I've never heard my mother profane a single thing. A good woman with a sense of propriety, she dutifully punished her children with Palmolive and Ivory Snow. Her maternal justice was called, "washing your mouth out with soap." For the most, it worked with me. I rarely swear. Though my wife might disagree with that.

All those Christmases ago

Every year, while I was teaching, on the last day of term, the Skolars played the graduating class in the annual end-of-semester hockey game. December 1984 was no exception. That year, I'd taken a leave of absence to acquire my Master's Degree at Western. My wife, our two sons and I, lived in married-students' residence on campus in London from Sunday evening through Thursday noon. On Thursdays, I picked up our sons at daycare, our dog at the in-law's, and drove to Brantford where Cathy was waiting at W. Ross MacDonald School for the Visually Impaired while she worked on her specialist in blind education, and from there drove to our home in Simcoe where tenant Guy Johnson was awaiting our arrival, on this occasion with a pizza, a belated birthday cake and the news that we were playing hockey that evening in preparation for Friday's Christmas game.

What prospects! Unfortunately, both of my sons were sick with stomach flu and had been entertaining their father for the past two hours by engaging in a game of tag-team puking in the car all the way home. To add insult to injury, daddy had been suffering excruciating gastro-intestinal agony due to a bug in the gut that had slimmed him down by a good ten pounds over the past seven days. I pulled into the driveway, the interior of the car reeking of vomit, I staggered into the house, crawled upstairs, and flopped down on the bed leaving Cathy to contend with our two ailing sons. Meanwhile, Guy stood in the pizza-fragrant kitchen with the frosted cake festooned with a tiny forest of unlit candles. Needless to say, I did not attend the game that night, nor did I play the following day.

I ended up in hospital connected to an IV drip, dehydrated, dejected, and discouraged. Even the enema was painful. However, by Christmas morning I had recovered and was feeling well enough to celebrate the opening of presents at home. Santa had been generous. That year Dylan being five and Sean three, St. Nick had seen fit to deliver ice skates to our address. For Dylan, a shiny new pair of Bauer hockey skates. For younger brother Sean, a toddler's pewter-coloured bob skates. I'd flooded the backyard that year, and Dylan, thrilled to receive the real thing, imagined himself flashing around the ice like a hockey star. Sean's reaction was far less enthusiastic, bordering on disastrous. My little three-year old son gripped those slipshod by the leather strap, spun them like nunchaku, and in one effective windmill motion flung them clattering into the corner scarring the wall on the way. Boxing day sales are for disappointed children. Sean wasn't a brat. He just knew, even at three years of age, that he didn't want those mortifying bob skates bound to his humbled shoe bottoms. He wanted authentic skates. Poor Sean. Though elder brother Dylan never truly caught the hockey bug, Sean would eventually become a very good hockey player. On the ice at Copps Coliseum in Hamilton he stripped the puck from NHL superstar Doug Gilmour during an exhibition game between the police and the NHL Oldtimers. Gilmour sent him to school for that, but Sean scored a goal, and he certainly wasn't wearing bob skates that day.

I love hockey that much

One morning I woke, as always of a winter Monday, expecting to play hockey that afternoon. But it had snowed all night and the drifts were three-foot deep on level ground. Elsewhere, they were banked to the threshold, banked to the windowsills, banked to the very eaves. At the time we lived in a house with detached garage. The driveway sloped to the street a hundred feet from car to curb. Pushing wide the kitchen door so the bottom rail scraped on crusted snow, I set out with my shovel and a sense of purpose. I'd already phoned the arena. Though the buses were canceled and the schools were closed, the rink remained open—an answered prayer. It took an hour to shovel a knee-deep path wide enough for a man and almost half a day to clear an area wide enough for my car to make its way from where it was parked and from there into the late-plowed streets. Some might curl up with a coffee and wile away lazy hours in an easy chair. Others might stoke a fire and read a good book. I'd have shoveled my way to the very parking lot. I'd have trudged that difficult distance with my equipment bag slung on my shoulder till the strapline burned. In those days I only played hockey once a week. Nothing would stop me from playing that day. I love hockey that much.

The winter before the birth of our children, I used to lace up, head out the door, cross the yard, climb the fence to play hockey alone with my dog in the moonlight. We lived next to a swamp that froze. Ebenezer and I would race through dogwood whippets that threaded the ice. I'd weave among the reeds and the red branches carrying the puck in the dark, barely able to see the night-blackened ice. He'd bark and chase and yelp if I skated on his tail. He'd yip for joy when he caught the puck then gather it up in his laughing mouth and run from the ice and off into deep snow where the puck was lost forever, dropping through, making a dark slot as it sank. I love hockey that much. I'd even play with a puck-stealing dog.

When our first son was a born I'd put on my skates, tuck baby Dylan into the snuggly, zip my parka surrounding him in the warm quilted lining of the coat, head out the door, climb the fence, and play hockey in that same swamp. I took special care not to stumble over weed stems and dogwood branches bristling on the surface of the ice. Ebenezer chased us through brambles and burdock barking with delight. I rarely took a stick or a puck, but I thrilled to feel my son's warm body sleeping close to my heart. I love hockey that much. I felt it in the heartbeat of my child, in the way we skated, his breath, my breath and the pure joy of winter on the outdoor ice of the swale.

One time on the way to hockey, I found myself driving through weather blind with snow. My destination was miles from home along a desolate highway. My windshield wiper motor quit and the blades went still. I'd blown a fuse. I refused to abandon the prospect of playing. Rolling down the window and clearing the glass with my naked hand, I drove the twenty kilometers to the rink. I played two hours and repeated the journey. All the way home, stopping every so often to sweep away the deep accumulations of snow from the arc of the glass. I love hockey that much.

Another evening, a fellow poet and I cut short an event in the city. He'd flown in from New Brunswick and I had organized a poetry reading for him and me. We'd drawn an audience of about one hundred enthusiastic listeners. The reading began at seven, and hockey began at eight-fifteen. We both read with one anxious eye on the clock. Laurence knew about the game in advance and he'd had brought his equipment on the plane. We sped through a few poems, sold a few books, shook a few grateful hands, engaged a few fans of our work in the perfunctory chit chat that occurs sometimes after a reading, and rushed out the door pages flying in our wake like a whirlwind in a school ground. We made it just in time for the second half of the game. Laurence leapt the boards, picked up the puck, skated for the net and scored. That was the best poetry reading of our life. He loves the game. And me, I'd rather play than read, I love hockey that much.

I've jumped the boards with a broken leg. I've taped up my hand and taken my shift with a splint on my finger. I've cracked my head and split my nose and snotted red ice. I've played with walking pneumonia all winter. I once drove an hour each way all summer to play in Norwich. I even gave serious consideration to joining my son in Toronto to play with his pick-up hockey team. I've played with my baby strapped to my belly. I've played with my shepherd mutt. I've played with the best. I've driven to Windsor to work all day, then driven home to play, and then turned around and driven back. And I'll play with you, if you ask, anytime, anywhere. I love the game that much.

In the end

Sadly, the guy who runs hockey finally gave our eldest player the word. "Davey, you're done," he'd said. Davey's eighty-seven, and he'd fallen all by his lonesome and hit his head cracking it hard on the ice and he'd taken a while to get up. When Bill came into the dressing room and gave Davey the bad news, you could have heard a sock drop. Everyone knew it was the right thing to do, but no one wanted it to be done. It broke hearts all round. Everyone sat there, half naked, staring at the floor. Saying nothing. When Bill said, "We're worried you'll hurt yourself, or worse, someone will run into you by accident and send you to the hospital." Davey quietly said, almost to himself, "It's my body." And then he said, "Well, can I at least finish out the year?" Bill replied, "Okay, Davey, but then that's it. You're done."

Davey's a sad case. He refuses to accept the fact that the time has come to hang up his skates and quit the game he loves. Delusional, almost a nonagenarian, he wobbles when he takes a stride. He toddles on the ice like a four-year old. Wherever he stands he totters on the spot like a bumped vase. The most common joke: "Draw a circle round him; see if he moves." I've seen him fall any number of times in the past few weeks. It's as though the thought of falling had simply crossed his mind. "I'm going to fall—NOW!" And a small tremor travels through his body from blade to helmet and *bang*, down he goes like a shot stag. I've read somewhere recently that the very young fall forward, and the very elderly fall backward. This is certainly the case with old Davey. His eyes wide, his balance gone, he topples backwards, cracking his helmet, letting his stick fly, as down he falls, flat out like a stunned snow angel. It's gotten to the point where most of us simply play on. One guy even said out loud, "Fuck 'im! If he doesn't know when to quit, just skate around him like he's a thin-ice pylon."

Davey recently told his grandkids, "I'm one of the best players out there." And then, when they came to see him play, one of them asked him afterwards, "Grampa, why doesn't anyone ever pass you the puck?"

"I don't know," he said. "They should, shouldn't they?" he mused, as if he wanted an answer. But he doesn't want an answer. He wants the game to love him the way he loves the game. And that just can't be so.

"You have to know that when people see what's happening with Davey, they see themselves in a year or two," Frank says. And he says it slow. Slow enough to sink in.

As if he were saying, "You know, no matter how much we love them, eventually we're going to have to eat the dogs."

A conversation gone awry

"There goes the best hockey player in the world!" he shouted through the rolled-down side window of his SUV as he drove past my wife and I while we were walking down Main Street in Dover.

"Hey!" I responded. "How've you been?"

"Is he delusional?" my wife inquired. She's always been an ego booster.

"I haven't seen that guy in years. We used to play together on Wednesday nights in Simcoe." I said as I sat on the bench in front of the pharmacy, opening the local newspaper to page four where my picture appeared accompanied by a story informing the community that I had won yet another poetry award.

I know she was only joking, but I find myself wishing, if only just for a moment that he might have meant it, that it might have been true.

"There goes the best hockey player in the world," he'd said. And that was me he was pointing to—living the dream—a comment overheard by passersby, strangers who, but for my wife's comment might have been left wondering—"Is it true? Is he really that good at something that matters?" Perhaps they were thinking such a thought, glancing over my shoulder, seeing my picture in the paper, thinking, "It's him, it's John B. Lee, the greatest hockey player in the world, the guy who writes poetry when he has nothing better to do with his time."

John B. Lee